The Occupationist

Dr Ajay Sati

NewDelhi • London

Dr. Ajay Sati

BLUEROSE PUBLISHERS
India | U.K.

Copyright © Ajay Sati 2025

All rights reserved by author. No part of this publication may be reproduced, stored in a retrieval system or transmitted in any form or by any means, electronic, mechanical, photocopying, recording or otherwise, without the prior permission of the author. Although every precaution has been taken to verify the accuracy of the information contained herein, the publisher assumes no responsibility for any errors or omissions. No liability is assumed for damages that may result from the use of information contained within.

BlueRoseOne Publishers takes no responsibility for any damages, losses, or liabilities that may arise from the use or misuse of the information, products, or services provided in this publication.

For permissions requests or inquiries regarding this publication, please contact:

BLUEROSE PUBLISHERS
www.BlueRoseONE.com
info@bluerosepublishers.com
+91 8882 898 898
+4407342408967

ISBN: 978-93-6452-312-7

First Edition: March 2025

Occupational concerns are existential

Everyone who works is prone to develop work-related illness in varying degrees depending on exposure to harmful agents at workplace. Globally, large industries have reasonable Occupational Health (OH) access while individuals, the self-employed and MSME (Micro Small Medium Enterprise) business owners have low to nil OH access.

It is estimated that around 20% of all GMP (general medical practice) consultations are work-related and I hope the blogs in this book will create awareness in everyone that illnesses could be work-related, and that the ways to resolve the work-related illnesses are different.

Volume – 2

(Contains select articles from www.occupationist.com from January to December 2023)

Read more articles at www.occupationist.com

We all work, so some of our illnesses could be work-related or occupational.

Dr Ajay Sati

Occupationist
(an expert in diseases and other concerns of occupations)

> Everyday 6500 workers die due to diseases they get at workplaces compared to 1000 workers who die due to work-related accidents and injuries.
>
> Prevention of work-related (occupational) injuries is a priority while prevention of occupational diseases are often neglected.

Occupational Health is a medical specialty that prevents work-related illnesses by controlling recognized hazards and identifying unrecognized hazards at workplace.

Occupational Health is preventive, proactive, prophylactic, and pre-emptive. Its goal is to proactively identify if there is a problem at work, workplace or due to working conditions before it affects health and reduce the risks to As Low As Reasonably Practicable (ALARP) to prevent or slow down any harm. By doing so, Occupational Health pre-empts any occupational disease that may lead to an unhealthy and an unpleasant situation subsequently.

> Everyone works, just everyone. Hence, we should be mindful that we too can be victims of work-related diseases, fatal or non-fatal, and act in time to prevent it.

Dedication

The book is dedicated to my parents who during my childhood inculcated empathy and respect towards all workers among many other things that were imparted to me as part of growing up. It is a coincidence that I ended up becoming a doctor preventing illnesses in workers; a medical specialty that goes by the name Occupational Health.

I also dedicate this book to the workers all over the world who become a part of the sad story of getting unwell due to work, workplace and working conditions (3Ws) that was compounded by lack of access to Occupational Health services.

Acknowledgements

I sincerely acknowledge all my teachers, seniors and patients who have taught me so much about life and medicine in the past four decades. In fact, they were my practical books.

I thank my parents to have given me freedom to do whatever I wanted. Even if they have left for heavenly abode decades ago, I am guided by what I learnt from them.

I am indebted to my wife Sumita who encouraged me to blog and my sons Avijit and Abhinit who supported to convert the blogs into a book.

My brothers Kailash, Lalit, Sanjay and Manoj who would share my blogs with a lot of their friends, a sincere thanks to dear brothers!

Finally, I thank my friends who encouraged me to convert some blogs from my website www.occupationist.com into a book.

About the Author

Dr Ajay Sati is a medical graduate of Grant Medical College & Sir J.J Group of Hospitals, Mumbai. He has post-graduate qualifications in Industrial Medicine from College of Physicians and Surgeons, Mumbai and online diplomas in workplace safety & health, and occupational hygiene.

He has experience of working in government, MNCs and Indian MNCs, both in India and abroad. He has advised several billion-dollars brownfield and greenfield projects for companies in India and abroad in areas of employee wellness and health, including Occupational Health and Social Health. He also has experience of setting up health infrastructure including management of emergencies in remote locations as well as fine tuning online medical consultations since 1994 while supervising health services in the oilfields of Middle East.

He was instrumental in the advising management to extend coverage of tar roads in the oilfields of deserts in the Middle East to reduce incidence of backache due to driving on muddy roads, to have green grass football fields in the desert to reduce injuries to employees playing the game after office hours and create well-lit lush gardens with a fountain to improve mental health in the otherwise boring living areas of the desert etc.

He also played a role in construction of permanent accommodation for contract workers instead of portacabins where even food was standardized.

He has been invited to talk on Wellness and Occupational Health topics at the Central Labor Institute, International Labor Organization, IIT-Bombay, various corporations and schools.

Dr Ajay Sati contributed to a book in 2018 titled '***Your guide for safe and nutritious food at the workplace (The Orange Book)***' sponsored by FSSAI (Food Safety and Standards Authority of India) that was meant for distribution to all offices and industries in India.

He is member of Indian Association of Occupational Health (India), International Commission on Occupational Health (Italy), Royal Society of Public Health (UK) and Rotary International.

Besides being an excellent communicator, he is a clinician, medical administrator and a patient listener.

Contents

Preface xi
Prologue xv
Pigeon feeding and its municipal ban in Mumbai: A step to improve respiratory health... 1
Sleep advice from a Governor: The solution may worsen the problem... 5
Fourth Industrial Revolution: Future of worker health, job safety and security amidst AI 9
How business owners impact worker health: A historical perspective!... 15
Tunnel trapped workers: From Occupational Safety to Occupational Health... 23
WHO launches a Commission to tackle loneliness.................... 29
Is your office as safe for your health as it looks? 37
Discrimination at workplace and high blood pressure 43
The 70-hour workweek: Should India work so much? 49
Occupational (Work-Related) health risks and sustainable energy transition... 55
Work-Life Balance: An ingredient to make better managers 61
Food and Water safety at workplace 67
Domestic Workers and Occupational Health........................... 73
Breaks while working: Good for health, wellbeing, performance, and safety 79
AI Systems at workplace: An emerging concern in worker health... 85
Fatigue amongst pilots: An Occupational Health and Safety concern... 91
Wellbeing at workplace: Survey of Indian employee 97
The future of work in extreme heat....................................... 101
Eye discomfort at workplace: Take steps now....................... 105

Can office design influence your health and wellbeing? 109
Preventing 'take-home toxins' from being taken from workplace 113
Occupational Health issues in call-centre workers.................. 117
Diversity and Inclusion in Occupational Health....................... 121
Air-conditioned truck drivers' cabin in India: An Occupational Health Initiative 125
AI, U & OI 129
Robots at workplace and mental health................................. 135
Managing your mental health is mostly about 'having a frank timely talk' 139
Gig economy and worker health.. 143
End of Covid pandemic is not an end to good habits it taught 147
Carbon Monoxide: a dangerous gas in homes, offices & factories.. 151
Toxic positivity at workplace.. 157
Kharghar heatwave deaths: seek Occupational Health advice too!... 163
All women Work: A brief history of work and their health..... 167
Making workplace disability-friendly 173
Work-Related (Occupational) Rheumatoid Arthritis 179
Work-life balance, politicians, and Occupational Health......... 183

Preface

Simple stated, Occupational Health (OH) is a medical specialty that deals with worker health. It deals with the effect of work on the health of workers as well as other concerns of occupations. We all work, so some of our diseases could be occupational (work-related).

Very few workers globally have access to OH services. In India, for example, it is only those few workers employed in large industries who have some access to OH depending on the understanding of the management and the expertise of the OH provider. Even if the OH provisions are in bits and pieces, it helps compared to an absence of any OH provision.

In small enterprises, the business owner usually works or has an office close to the area where the workers work. Hence, business owners of small enterprises should be mindful that they can also be victims of some of the work-related (occupational) illnesses that a worker gets. That is why by improving workplace and working conditions, the business owners will also benefit as work-related illnesses they could have gotten are prevented due to initiatives taken to prevent work-related illnesses in their workers.

We all work and hence have to be very careful as it may surprise many of you that everyday around 6500 workers die globally due to the diseases they get at workplaces, compared to 1000 workers who die due to work-related accidents and injuries. The chances of death in a worker are about 6 times higher due to diseases that can be acquired at workplace than due to accidents or injuries. Despite these numbers, prevention of work-related (occupational) injuries is a high priority agenda with organizations with huge budget while prevention of occupational diseases at workplace is on a shoe-string budget or is often neglected.

Occupational Safety (OS) is better understood compared to Occupational Health (OH). And for some large enterprise employers, both are interchangeable words, while in reality they are not. OS and OH do cross roads but they are distinct; precisely the reason why OS is managed by Safety professionals (usually engineers) while OH is managed by medical professionals (doctors and/or nurses).

Also, it is a mistaken belief that establishing OH practices are necessary only in factories and that the office workers cannot get any work-related illnesses. Hence, most of the office-based businesses rarely seek inputs from OH physicians as a result the work-related illness of office-based workers like the IT and computer engineers, the bankers etc. goes unnoticed.

Globally, every year, 160 million (16 crore) workers are victims of Occupational Illness (OI). It can be safely assumed that the number in India must be high enough for action. Yet, everyone seems to be oblivious about it or are blind to it despite the numbers it kills or is a cause for an illness, sometimes irreversible.

Many illnesses among workers are treated without a successful outcome because work, workplace or working conditions (3Ws) are not taken into consideration. An illness that is work-related can be successfully treated only if the 3Ws are accounted for. For example, a work-related backache is treated differently than a backache that is not work-related. A work-related backache may not just require medications but modifications around the 3Ws for a successful outcome, else the backache recurs once the medications are stopped as it is the 3Ws which are contributing to the backache that have not been rectified.

An awareness among employers and workers that an illness can occur due to the work that I am doing is not only important but is urgent too. Awareness is important because the way an Occupational Illness is managed is different than the usual approach of treatment. Awareness is urgent because of the number of workers getting occupational illnesses are increasing. At 160 million OI cases globally annually, the world has waited enough. It can't wait any more. It's time governments intervene.

Globally, around 160 million were victims of Occupational Illness of which 2.1 million died, yet there was little attention from most governments or private enterprises.

There are around 3000 OH professionals in India, the majority of whom are employed by large, medium or small organised industries. Of these only a few are full-time employees, the others being employed part-time to meet the compliance of the Factories Act. An estimated 380 million (38 crore) of India's workforce is employed in the unorganised sector (construction, fishing, gig workers etc.) who do not have any access to OH services and they themselves as well as their employers have no awareness that the work that they are doing can also affect their health and lead serious illnesses and eventually premature death. Of course, the situation is no different in many developing countries as well as in developed countries as the OH professionals are in short supply.

Efforts by organizations are to prevent instant death due to accidents and injuries (worker safety) while slow death due to work, workplace or working conditions (worker health) is often neglected by the management.

Prevention of accidents gets priority because of multiple reasons, one of them being it is reported by the media; secondly, it instantly kills; third, it obviously implies to the workers and common public alike that something was inherently wrong with systems and so has reputational risks.

Occupational diseases kill slowly, over years at times, are poorly understood by the learned as well as the common man, and there is no media coverage; hence the reputational risks are low. However, higher incidence of Occupational Illnesses in office workers may lead to higher attrition and indirectly harm reputations. Hence, it is time that employers and business owners understand the significance of establishing OH practices at workplace, not just in factories for the sake of compliance but in offices to be morally correct.

Unless the workers, and we all are in some form or the other, have the awareness and realize that **'my health problem could be because of the work I do'**, prevention of work-related (occupational) disease will never be understood and occupational illness will keep rising. The employers should also realize that they are workers too, and are prone to work-related illnesses and should take steps themselves too to minimize the risk.

One of the emerging concerns in Occupational Health is AI; the other being use of robots. By now we all know about the positives of AI and robots but not yet about all its negatives as the applications are recent. An eye should be kept on any new negative impact AI and robots can have on health and mitigation strategies put in place. Some negative impacts have been identified and mitigation suggested. Industries involved in AI research and application should be mindful of these. Likewise, industries installing robots should carefully choose to avoid both its impact on worker health and the unrest it can create in society.

Dr Ajay Sati
1 June, 2024
Mumbai, India

Prologue

I write blogs on Occupational Health to help many of those employees and employers who have minimal or nil access to Occupational Health physicians (or Occupationist as I like to call myself). In fact, the world is full of people who have minimal to nil access to manage work-related (occupational) issues.

Why is it important for everyone to know about Occupational Health? It is simply because a lot of times the illness could be due to the work the individual is doing, the workplace in which the person is working or the working conditions around; and hence an understanding of it sometimes makes it easier to treat the illness.

It has always intrigued me about how to make available OH advice to millions of disadvantaged workers and even employers (who are compassionate but don't know how to) all over the world who have no access to doctors or nurses specializing in Occupational Health. This is also because occupational illnesses are increasing – it is a wake-up call; left alone it could lead to industrial relations issues (labour unrest), litigations and a scarcity for businesses to get skilled workers.

After decades of working in various large corporations and interacting with people from all walks of life, an in-depth definition of Occupational Health as I view it is as follows:

Occupational Health is a preventive, proactive, prophylactic, and pre-emptive medical specialty. Its goal is to proactively identify if there is a problem at work, workplace or due to working conditions before it affects health of the worker and reduce the risks to as low as reasonably practicable (ALARP). By doing so, it prevents the spread or occurrence of occupational (work-related) illness or slows down any harm in more than one worker doing similar jobs in the designated work area and pre-empts any occupational disease by taking an appropriate action in time to avert an unhealthy and an unpleasant situation subsequently, both for the employee as well as the employer.

Given the lack of understanding of the issue (that work can cause illness) and paucity of OH physicians it is impossible that even in the next hundred years Occupational Health advice will reach the workers who need them the most. Hence, in the absence of access to OH professionals, the employers should be mindful of the 5As and talk about the 5As with the employees as was discussed in Volume-1, and is briefly reproduced below.

Individuals, the self-employed and MSMEs who do not have access to OH services have an endless wait to resolve the work-related health issues they happen to see in their workers. What they can do is understand and remember the 5A approach and use it to resolve simple, nagging work-related health issues themselves. How does the 5A approach help manage some of the work-related discomfort or illness at a basic level? As a first step, the individual develops **'Awareness'** by interacting with the environment (including the work environment) that work can harm health, **'Act'** is instinctive, **'Adapt'** is reasoning, **'Adopt'** is acceptance and **'Adhere'** is discipline.

Having **'awareness'** that 'my health problem could be because of the work I do' is the first step. Some workers **act** instinctively when faced with a health issue and if the action taken helps; they reason it out to **adapt** it. They continue using the steps taken and **adopt** it in their daily routine of work and accept it as by now they realize that it works for them. They know if they discontinue the self-approved interventions, the symptoms may recur, so they **adhere** to the new practice that they have adopted.

Most of the time it works and resolves the misery of the worker. The 5A approach is a natural step that people take if there is a thought that the work (job) I do can harm my health.

As an example regarding the 5A approach, I often cite the story of an autorickshaw (the black and yellow 3-wheeler) driver in Mumbai. When the autorickshaw driver passes through the dusty lanes, he/she notices that it is the dust that is causing the symptoms of running nose, itchy eyes which is becoming chronic. This is *'awareness'* in the driver that my health problem is because of the dust. The instinctive *'act'* is to either tie a handkerchief or use a mask. Wearing a mask helps, so they *'adapt'* it for a new purpose. Since wearing a mask helps, they embrace it or *'adopt'* it in their daily routine. By now they know that if they leave their self-approved interventions, the symptoms may recur; so, they *'adhere'* to it. This is how a worker can prevent to some extent the illnesses in the absence of access to OH physician.

The 5A approach was born out of my concern and worry for the individual, the self-employed and workers employed in MSME who are unlikely to get access to OH services in their lifetime and may have to live with the nagging work-related health problem, some of which they could have resolved themselves.

I talk about the 5A approach to the public as well as to workers who have no OH access. I propose businesses owners who do not have access to OH physicians also talk about it to their workers. OH is mainly preventative, but is also curative; only that the method to manage or resolve work-related health issues are different. And in the absence of access to OH services, the 5A approach helps in not only preventing a disease in a worker but also arrests its progression to something more serious.

From the business owners' point of view, Occupational Health (OH) at a basic level requires ACW, that is, **alertness**, **compassion**, and **willingness**. Alertness identifies a problem of the worker, compassion is about understanding the suffering faced, and willingness is the action taken to alleviate the suffering. As an example, Ratan Tata did exactly that – he demonstrated alertness by identifying the problem the workers were having during his visit to the Tata-owned car factory, had compassion towards the suffering of the workers when he said, 'How can we expect our men to do this throughout their lives? Surely it will damage their health,' and finally exhibited willingness by calling his mangers and saying, 'We must provide an automation solution on priority.' The Tata engineers took the challenge and did the needful thus making the workers work more comfortable.

The blogs in Volume-2 create awareness on various aspects of work, workplace and working conditions and what the enterprises can do in absence of access to OH services which are scarce globally. When services are scarce, people either face the brunt on their quality of life or find ways to get relief, one of which could be to consider the 5As.

As I see nothing in sight that can provide OH access to majority of workers globally in the near future, unless a humanoid OH physician is made available by the governments, the best way out is to talk about the 5As and the ACW as described above so that some of the work-related illnesses can be prevented. In this era of social media and litigations, it becomes even important to prevent any work-related illness from taking an unhealthy and an unpleasant situation, both for employee and the employer.

1

Pigeon feeding and its municipal ban in Mumbai: A step to improve respiratory health

(published on 31st December, 2023 in www.occupationist.com)

Finally, in December 2023, the BMC (Brihanmumbai Municipal Corporation) imposed a ban on pigeon feeding in Mumbai city. What should have been done decades ago will eventually give solace to a lot of citizens. A ban, well in time would have prevented thousands of lungs from irreversible damage due to inhalation of pigeon droppings (poop, shit). Sad, it is always the few who create most of the problems.

Animals and birds have been designed to feed themselves; if they don't get food, they migrate.

The BMC will impose a fine, albeit, a meek one, and the believers in pigeon feeding may well pay the paltry 500 rupees fine. This is because some believe that pigeon feeding brings prosperity, though I have not heard of any businessman becoming prosperous because of pigeon feeding. Else there would be no poverty in this world – just feeding the pigeons a few grains would have done the trick.

Every life in this world is self-sufficient, except the human race. Animals and birds have been designed to feed themselves; if they don't get food, they migrate. It is only the humans who have to work. Even after migration, humans, in the quest of better living, often work hard to feed self and the family. The majority of migrants continue to live a difficult life which is precisely the reason why many charities and some governments feed their extremely poor citizens.

No government feeds animals or birds unless they are captivated and kept in the zoos. There is no government scheme to feed stray dogs or for that matter, the pigeons. If feeding pigeons made individuals prosper, governments of many third world nations would have encouraged just that.

Birds, including pigeons, and stray animals should not be fed for the above reasons – that they can feed themselves. Feeding them makes them lazy and dependent on you, eventually hovering around the feeding places and becoming a nuisance to the society by their droppings and shedding small feathers, both of which are bad for respiratory health of people exposed to it.

Until a decade ago, hypersensitivity pneumonitis (HP) was found in workers who worked as veterinary doctors (doctors who specialize in diseases of animals), or who worked as cleaners in kabutar khanas (places in Mumbai where pigeons are fed in large numbers) or in people who fed birds or lived near kabutar khanas.

But now people from all walks of life are getting HP. The Pulmonologists (Chest Physician) in Mumbai have seen a 5-fold increase in the number of cases of HP, and the common link is exposure to pigeon dropping.

Hypersensitivity pneumonitis (HP) causes permanent scarring of the lung tissue leading to breathing difficulties, eventually requiring 24/7 oxygen support or lung transplant.

When pigeon droppings dry, they become airborne and if inhaled, lead flu-like symptoms, pneumonia etc. Long-term exposure leads to irreversible damage to the lungs and poor respiratory health that keeps on worsening.

Diseases due to pigeon droppings used to be an occupational (work-related) illness; it still is, but is also becoming a major public health issue.

The ban on pigeon feeding is a welcome move as it will improve human health. According to KM Chandrashekar, assistant professor of Veterinary Microbiology at the Veterinary College, Hassan, Karnataka, India, pigeons carry parasites, ticks and fleas in their droppings and can spread up to 60 diseases in people exposed to dust from dried droppings.

Earlier diseases due to birds were found mainly in veterinary doctors and the support staff handling the birds. It was a work-related (occupational) illness. With increase in bird feeding, people who are not involved in handling the birds, but living in the vicinity are getting serious lung problems (requiring external oxygen and even lung transplant), making it a public health issue as well.

The pigeons carry parasites, ticks and fleas in their droppings and can spread up to 60 diseases in people exposed to the dust from the dried droppings. Many of these diseases are difficult and expensive to treat.

Some of the other serious diseases that people exposed to bird dropping, especially pigeon droppings are Histoplasmosis, Cryptococcosis, Candidiasis, Psittacosis, Avian tuberculosis, besides causing bird flu. All these diseases are difficult and even expensive to treat. Hence preventing it is not only better than cure but even cheaper.

Protecting your lungs from pigeon dropping:

As an Occupational Health physician, I would suggest the following to protect your lungs from being damaged permanently due to pigeon (and other bird's) droppings:

1. Stop feeding the birds. People should realize feeding birds doesn't bring prosperity; it only brings misery and ill-health
2. Citizens should intervene to stop those feeding the birds and educate them about its harm; and report to the authorities if they don't listen and continue to feed the birds
3. Do not let the dropping accumulate; keep cleaning the droppings taking precautions to protect oneself
4. Do not sweep the dried bird droppings; they become airborne and gain easy access to the lungs along with the air we breathe
5. Clean the bird droppings by making them wet with water or a disinfectant. This prevents droppings from becoming airborne so that people escape the 60 diseases that it can cause
6. Wear gloves, shoe coverings, masks (preferably N95) while cleaning the droppings
7. After the droppings are cleaned, they should be collected and stored in bags which must be sealed. The outside of the bag should be washed with water before disposing in designated areas
8. Have nets to minimize exposure to birds and their droppings
9. If passing through an area having pigeon droppings, make sure you wear a N-95 mask
10. While installing ACs, especially window AC, make sure there is no space for pigeons to rest near or below it

The ban on pigeon feeding by the municipality in Mumbai is a progressive step that will improve the respiratory health of its citizens! The State has done its job; now it is peoples' turn to do theirs and the 10 steps outlined above should help.

2

Sleep advice from a Governor: The solution may worsen the problem

(published on 15th December, 2023 in www.occupationist.com)

On 5th December 2023, a governor of a State (province) in India urged the Education Department to consider change in school timings so that students could catch up with sleep.

I was wondering, that even if the advice was right, the solution was such that it could worsen the problem.

> ***Smartphones can cause a lot of health issues and hence smartphones should be handled smartly.***

Delaying school timings will only encourage students to spend even more time with the smartphone. Overuse of electronic devices at night is known to disrupt sleep patterns. In fact, health experts recommend that television, smartphones, toys having lights etc. should not be in children's bedroom during sleep hours to ensure sound sleep.

Overuse of smartphones not only interferes with sleep but can also cause eye strain, tech neck, text thumb etc. Hence smartphones should be handled smartly.

A disrupted sleep in a student is a recipe for academic disaster just as sleep deficit in a worker can lead to industrial disaster (gas leaks, nuclear accidents etc.). A sportsperson who had a disturbed sleep can lose a match (tournament).

In addition, students with chronic insufficient sleep are more likely to demonstrate feelings of hopelessness, loneliness, exhaustion, anxiety, and desire to self-harm. Students with chronic sleep deficit are also overweight or obese and more likely to feel depressed. Hence, advice should be to sleep well.

> ***The act of a child going to a school or a college to study is no less than an adult going to a workplace to do a job (work). The child is engaged in the act of 'occupation of studying' now for an 'occupation for wages' in future.***

A sleep deprived person usually has low academic or work performance. A sleepy student is a sloppy student just as a sleepy worker is a sloppy worker.

Sleep is very important. In fact, some of the CEOs of USA these days often emphasize that sleep should be given priority over diet and exercise in a wellness program. The irony is that sleep is hardly talked about in most wellness programs. Instead of wellness initiatives starting with diet and exercise, it should start with sleep as it is as basic a need.

> ***A sleepy student is a sloppy student just as a sleepy worker is a sloppy worker.***

Wellness initiatives in corporations talking about work-life balance should focus on sleep emphasizing that sleep is a basic need to recover and rejuvenate.

Sleep leadership in the corporate world is all about encouraging sleep among workers by senior managers.

The act of a child going to a school or a college to study is no less than an adult going to a workplace to do a job (work). The child is engaged in the act of *'occupation of studying'* now for an *'occupation for wages'* in future.

Children going to school or college to study can be considered to be engaged in a unique occupation as their workplace (school/college) is not bound by any legal healthcare requirements.

Hence, sleep leadership must be introduced in schools and colleges where students should be told about benefits of good sleep as it leads to improvement in critical thinking, creativity, relationships, performance and general health. Sleep time of at least 7-8 hours should be encouraged among students as it is a good recovery tool that helps rebuild the body and mind. Sleep leadership in schools will help the younger generation of workers in future work efficiently.

Sleep incentives does help in making people get more sleep. At health insurance Aetna, employees who can prove (using Fitbit data or other means) that they've had a good night's sleep can receive a per-night monetary incentive.

Sleep leadership must be introduced in schools and colleges as it will help the younger generation of workers in future work efficiently.

If you have a morning school, the old saying 'early to bed, early to rise' is a statement that most students will find useful. Using smartphone for academic activities or information seeking is a good thing to do. However, engaging in social media apps may not be beneficial as it sucks away a lot of your valuable study time.

Some schools and colleges employ doctors to advise them on health affairs. In USA, there are universities having an Occupational Health department employing doctors and nurses. The doctors in such schools, colleges and universities having such a facility should demonstrate sleep leadership and encourage students to have 7-8 hours of sleep.

A Governor of a State (province) in India has a panel of doctors for advice on personal and other matters. If the Governor had an Occupational Health (OH) physician as part of the panel, the statement would have been different rather than urging the Education Department to consider change in school timings so that students could catch up with sleep.

Governments would greatly benefit if they empanel an OH physician in their team of health advisors for appropriate inputs of many such opinions and advisories due to their experience in proactively managing health of various occupations.

And when there is no support of doctors or an Occupational Health department, 'sleep leadership' in such situations becomes 'sleep discipline', as you are your own leader!

With the workforce increasingly being dominated by millennials and Gen-Z, 'sleep leadership' will find a platform soon in organizations where it hasn't; that's the future and that's one of the solutions which leaders will find it difficult to ignore to improve performance!

3

Fourth Industrial Revolution: Future of worker health, job safety and security amidst AI

(published on 8th December, 2023 in www.occupationist.com)

We are witnessing IR 4.0 (the 4th industrial revolution) and Artificial Intelligence (AI), an often-heard term these days is a part of it. AI is still in its infancy, and as perceived by workers, a robot is its partner in crime. We yet don't know its capabilities. The experts are harnessing its potential and the common man is worried about losing their jobs, job security of future generations as well as its effect on health, both physical and mental.

AI-based technology is no less than a nuclear bomb in wrong hands and deepfake is like a dirty bomb in the hands of miscreants.

In the future of jobs, no one knows who will win and who will lose. Job safety may improve due to AI and other IR 4.0 technologies, however, at the moment not much has been thought about its impact on the health of workers – both physical and mental.

It is important to bear in mind that AI is a ruthless tool devoid of human emotions. It has no idea about compassion. It cannot empathize. Hence, before marketing the goodness of AI for the public, one should think about its public and societal harms. No technology should create ill-health and unrest in society.

Before 2014, if you searched the term "Industry 4.0" in Google, it was practically non-existent, but everything changed around 2019 with Covid giving a big kick to IR 4.0 to gallop where it is today! The salient features of IR 4.0 are improved connectivity, advanced analytics, automation, robotics, complex engineering and technology for cheaper, better, faster manufacturing etc.

AI is still in its infancy, and as perceived by workers, a robot is its partner in crime.

In 2006, the Boliden's Garpenberg zinc mine, near Stockholm in Sweden where mining is happening since 375 B.C., was struggling to compete. In 2013 Boliden started transforming its operations with automation and data, and is now one of the world's most productive zinc mines. They also employ robots for mining.

Jenny Gotthardsson, general manager at Garpenberg said, "We have a way to go. There's a big possibility of working 24 hours a day with more automation." Some of the workers will be retrained for the new high-tech jobs but full automation will reduce jobs overall. Kristofer Ruth, a miner who has worked for 11 years, rarely goes to the mines. He manipulates a joystick that shovels ore into an automated truck about 800 metres below.

The worker may be safe with better health and safety at work due to AI but is not sure if the job will continue. The worker is not only concerned about the present job but also of jobs for future generations. Hence, there may be opposition from trade unions while implementing technologies associated with IR 4.0.

In future it is possible that IR 4.0 technologies will be able to prevent work-related (occupational) illnesses; for example, it may prevent musculoskeletal disorders by wearing a robot that will support human strength.

Deep-learning algorithm may help to detect human behavior patterns by using security cameras. If a dangerous situation is recognized, the relevant system can alert the operator and the safety team immediately to prevent an accident.

The worker may be safe with better health and safety at work due to AI but is not sure if the job will continue. Any increase in employment instability can increase mental illness.

IR 4.0 will accelerate globalization and consequently the working conditions.

Globalization increases night shift working, especially in developing countries. Shift work disrupts circadian rhythm and increases the risk of certain cancers (colorectal and breast), stroke, heart attacks, depression and even diabetes.

Shift workers tend to eat more erratically, snack more at night and consume a lot more unhealthy foods with more calories as per a study published online in *Advances in Nutrition*.

To minimize circadian rhythm disturbances, it is necessary to maintain a normal biological clock by taking the following steps:

- Reduce light exposure as much as possible after leaving work if intending to go immediately to sleep once at home. Wearing blue light-blocking glasses or using blackout shades in your bedroom is helpful, says Eric Zhou, an assistant professor in the Division of Sleep Medicine at Harvard Medical School.
- On days off, make enough time for sleep
- Have a consistent shift work schedule
- Talk to your line manager/employer requesting to schedule for fewer overnight shifts. "You can also ask your doctor to make a case for you to be moved off these shifts or have more flexibility," Zhou says.

Zhou further says, "The goal is to preserve as strong a circadian rhythm as possible under the abnormal schedule shift work requires."

AI causes other issues like stress due to fear of losing jobs to robots or other complex systems. Any increase in employment instability can increase mental illness.

AI is a ruthless tool devoid of human emotions. Before marketing the goodness of AI for the public, one should think about its public and societal harms.

AI leads to platform companies and workers register in more than one such company as they do not have a fixed job. These jobs are on-demand and workers are not protected by labor laws in most countries. To protect health and wellbeing of such workers (also called gig workers), government intervention and enforcement is necessary.

Role of Occupational Health to manage work-related health fallouts due to IR 4.0?

- Make a case for implementing the latest versions of decent work in corporations. The global bodies defining decent work should change the definition of decent work based on ongoing research.
- Aggressive focus on identifying and preventing work-related diseases rather than on treatment as in some cases treatment may not be effective.
- Strong advocacy with the governments to be quick to frame labor-friendly laws and enforce them to protect worker health.

The difference between Human Intelligence (HI) and AI is the latter's inability to discern and judge. And that is why OHS (Occupational Health and Safety) professionals must demonstrate compassion, empathy and ability to make rightful decisions based on experience and situational awareness, else AI will take over a large part of OHS.

In short, OHS will have to anticipate, innovate and coordinate to be relevant in the years to come.

The technologies of the fourth industrial revolution (IR 4.0) which includes AI can be dangerous in wrong hands as it can terrorize communities and equally dangerous in right hands if its societal harms are not accounted before its implementation. The societal harms are increase in joblessness and health issues (both physical and mental) in those working with AI systems.

AI-based technology is no less than a nuclear bomb in wrong hands and deepfake is like a dirty bomb in the hands of miscreants.

Hence, the expectations from governments are to urgently have a global framework of understanding to monitor ethical and transparent development of AI and other such technologies and have strong enforcement regarding its misuse, much like the regulatory boards for nuclear energy.

The happiness because of achievements due to AI now should not turn into societal chaos in future and lead to dangerous conflicts. Regulations are important and are urgently required.

India is among the top countries in AI applications and research. While being a part of global framework to develop standards, India must voice concerns and prevent any application of AI that can disrupt physical and mental health as the cost of managing them in a populous country far outweighs the gains.

4

How business owners impact worker health: A historical perspective!

(published on 4th December, 2023 in occupationist.com)

History is proof to many business owners taking steps to prevent illnesses and accidents in workers either due to compassion or to be seen as a good employer. History is proof also to ruthless business owners with scant regard to worker health.

There are no records or stories of worker health during ancient civilizations. Massive structures were made using stone and other mixtures. A lot of carving on stones was also done. All this in an era when there was no knowledge that work can harm health; and perhaps there were no gloves, masks etc. One can only imagine the state of worker health. Hundreds of years ago, the kings and the rich were the big business owners.

The situation of worker health is no different even now, more in the unorganised sectors but a lot needs to be done in the organised sectors as well, especially the banking and IT industry. One of the reasons is lack of awareness that work can harm health.

Mining was a big business before the industrial revolution (1760 AD). Hippocrates (460-377 B.C), whose famous Hippocratic Oath taken by medical students world-wide, contributed to field of Occupational Health (worker health) by describing symptoms of lead poisoning in miners and metallurgists.

Paracelsus (1493 AD to 1541 AD), a Swiss physician described lung diseases among miners and attributed it to vapours that originated from metals.

Agricola (1494 AD to 1555 AD) was a physician appointed to the mining town of Jochimstral in the Swiss mountains. He Wrote *De Re Metallica*, a comprehensive discourse addressing every aspect of mining, smelting and refining. He noted the need to provide ventilation for miners, and described "asthma" among workers who toiled in dusty mines. Agricola wrote, "Some mines are so dry that they are entirely devoid of water and this dryness causes the workmen even greater harm, for the dust, which is stirred and beaten up by digging, penetrates into the windpipe and lungs, and produces difficulty in breathing and the disease the Greeks call asthma. If the dust has corrosive qualities, it eats away the lungs and implants consumption in the body. In the Carpathian mountains women are found who have married seven husbands, all of whom this terrible consumption has carried off to a premature death."

History is proof also to ruthless business owners with scant regard to worker health.

Bernardino Ramazzini - 1633-1714, an Italian physician, whose book *De Morbis Artificium Diatriba* (The Diseases of Workmen) described the symptoms of mercury and lead poisoning and other occupational diseases. He wrote about the pathology of silicosis and recommended precautions to avoid hazards. He also advised physicians to learn about occupational diseases by studying the work environment, and persuaded them to always ask patients "Of what trade are you?" or simply stated "what is your occupation". Ramazzini is aptly called as the father of industrial (occupational) medicine.

During IR 1.0 (Industrial Revolution 1.0) which was the start of Industrial revolution in 1760 AD, workers were treated no less than slaves. There are some recorded incidents which are indicative of total disregard for worker health, both men and women.

Rapid industrialization led to overcrowding of towns. For example, population in The Port of Liverpool increased exponentially in a short span of time. Diseases were rampant. Science was not as advanced as it is today, so, people didn't know what was going wrong. The governing (business) classes who lived in different areas never saw these conditions, and protests from the workers were ignored, says Wilde, Robert in his article "Public Health During the Industrial Revolution." ThoughtCo, Apr. 5, 2023, thoughtco.com/public-health-in-the-industrial-revolution-1221641.

In 1832, one doctor said only 10% of Leeds (UK) was in full health. Tuberculosis, typhus, and after 1831, cholera was rampant. The 1842 report by the British social reformer Edwin Chadwick called "Report on the Sanitary Condition of the Labouring Population of Great Britain" showed that the life expectancy of an urban dweller was less than that of a rural one.

The terrible working environments created new occupational hazards, such as lung disease and bone deformities.

The first Public Health act was passed in 1848 based on the recommendations of a Royal Commission and Chadwick was among others was also appointed to the board. The act is considered to have failed as the death rate remained the same, and the problems remained, but it did establish a precedent for government intervention as opposed to laissez-faire system in which governments didn't interfere in the lives of adult men. Chadwick was disliked and some wags in the government claimed they preferred cholera to him.

History is proof to many business owners taking steps to prevent illnesses and accidents in workers either due to compassion or to be seen as a good employer.

In 1875 Prime Minister Benjamin Disraeli who was not a businessman, passed several acts aimed at social improvements, such as a new Public Health Act and an Artisan's Dwellings Act. A Food and Drink Act was passed to attempt to improve diet. These acts marked the beginning of a genuine, workable public health strategy, with responsibility shared between the local and national government, and the death rate finally began to fall.

In India, as early as 1895, Jamsetji Tata, a prominent businessman, while speaking at the opening of a new extension of Empress Mills, Jamsetji Tata talked about some of the specific steps that Empress Mills had taken for employee care. For instance, on the subject of ventilation in the mills, Jamsetji said, 'we have paid the greatest attention to sanitary arrangements, and constantly studied the question with the view to improve them.'

Tata further said, 'we have provided fans for ventilation, humidifiers to prevent the effects of extremely dry air, khus-khus tatties for cooling the rooms, which must, by the nature of our business, get hotter in the hot weather. But still we are not satisfied with what we have done.' Continuing his address, Jamsetji said, 'We are about to try a new scheme in the shed. This scheme, we hope, will be a great improvement upon what we have hitherto done, and we are confident that if it succeeds in nothing else, it is sure to succeed in one thing – and that is in giving an equally distributed supply of free, fresh and pure air to our workpeople.'

This was a profound speech by Jamsetji Tata, and a great thought process in Occupational Health (OH) and Industrial Hygiene (IH) in India almost 145 years ago. Even the developed world then wasn't as compassionate to the workers and were struggling to lay down the fundamentals of OH and IH.

Business owners not having a strong commitment to worker health will appear to their employees, the peers and the public like the cruel and self-centered mine-operators of the 15th century.

An incident relating to a coffee break in 1968 led Sidney Harman, cofounder of Harman Kardon music systems to revamp the factory and its working and turned it into a kind of college campus offering classes in the factory premises including piano lessons. Prior to revamping, the factory was in Harman's words, raw, ugly and in many ways demeaning.

Revamping the factory by Harman also meant providing safer and better working conditions to the workers resulting in fewer work-related illnesses and accidents.

Harman not only became a leader but somewhere unknowingly he also introduced good practice of occupational health as the era of sweat shops was long over and he must have viewed the coffee break as an important link between worker health and work performance. The workers were encouraged to take most of the responsibility to run the workplace.

How pathetic it is for a child to see a parent come home from work looking sick and/or dying a slow death due to the nature of work done. Establishing OH practices can undo that to a large extent.

Ratan Tata's contribution to Occupational Health in the Indica car factory in 1996-97 is one of awareness, compassion and willingness. Ratan Tata had noticed the operators fix the rear strut of the car manually and would have to bend down 600 times to complete this operation on 300 cars each day. He had called his managers and asked, 'how can we expect our men to do this throughout their lives? Surely it will damage their health. We must provide an automation solution on priority.' The engineering department rose to the occasion and quickly developed a fixture to semi-automate the operation.

Around April 2009, by getting the goats to mow the lawns and remove the brush (dry grass), Google did a master stroke of using principles of Occupational Health, albeit, unknowingly, by taking care of employee wellness, environmental health (air and noise pollution), social responsibility (local communities) and compliance of California laws to remove excess brush to reduce any chance of brush fires.

Google said that the cost of hiring 200 goats is about the same price as mowing, but the goats were "a lot cuter to watch." While the intent was to contribute to reducing noise and air pollution without affecting the cost, Google unknowingly contributed to employee wellness and happiness by stating that goats were a lot cuter to watch.

Not to be outdone, rival company Yahoo tweeted at Google saying, 'they like our grass too.' with a link of goats grazing on Yahoo properties in Sunnyvale.

Similarly, many companies have a fish tank in their offices or a small garden or a cozy sit out – these are good for employee health. It is another matter that most companies do it for the sake of making the office look attractive, contemporary and upmarket. Usually, such initiatives are done by the companies out of their own accord and often not knowing that it is contributing to employee health and wellness. That's the power of Occupational Health – it is omnipresent and small changes usually bring about big changes, by anyone; not necessarily by a OH physician.

I sometimes feel that Occupational Health (OH) at a basic level requires alertness, compassion, and willingness. Alertness identifies a problem of the worker, compassion is about understanding the suffering faced, and willingness is the action taken to alleviate the suffering. If employers or senior managers exhibit alertness, compassion, and willingness to situations at workplace during their walkthrough rounds or from inputs by an OH physician, a lot can be done and achieved in the arena of OH (occupational health) and eventually in protecting worker health.

If personal health is important and public health necessary, then Occupational Health is both, important and necessary. This is because only OH has the ability to mitigate illnesses due to work (Occupational Illnesses) which is still killing millions every year. The irony is that OH is neglected knowing well that we all work and it could affect all of us too.

Companies not having a strong commitment to worker health will appear to their employees, the peers and the public like the cruel and self-centered mine-operators of the 15th century.

No work is safe – it must be made safe, and every stakeholder, including business owners must work towards it. Even if practices of OH are established initially in bits and pieces, it can go a long way in improving worker health.

How pathetic it is for a child to see a parent come home from work looking sick and/or dying a slow death due to the nature of work done. Establishing OH practices can undo that to a large extent.

Tunnel trapped workers: From Occupational Safety to Occupational Health

(published on 30th November, 2023 in www.occupationist.com)

On Sunday, 12th November 2023, at around 5.30 AM IST, a portion of the Silkyara Bend - Barkot tunnel, under construction, collapsed in the Uttarkashi district of the state of Uttarakhand, India. 41 workers got trapped inside the tunnel.

On Tuesday, 28th November, after 17 days, all the 41 trapped workers were rescued. This was possible due to a constant vigil being kept on the efforts by various agencies. It was a victory for India's disaster management expertise.

As soon as the news of the workers trapped in a tunnel was out, highest level rescue operations under the title Operation Zindagi was immediately launched by Government of India, which was led by the National Disaster Response Force (NDRF), the State Disaster Response Force (SDRF), and the police.

What looked like an occupational safety (OS) issue initially, overlapped and became an occupational health (OH) issue as well because of the delay in getting the workers out due to operational reasons. If the rescue would have been completed in a day or two, it would have been a safety issue alone, and perhaps not much of an OH issue.

Accidents happen despite the best of precautions taken. In an accident, either the people involved die, get maimed or develop severe PTSD (post trauma stress disorder).

In this Silkyara tunnel collapse, the 41 workers have been in artificial light supplied from outside, food, medicines and oxygen are being sent via a duct, and doctors and others senior government officials have come to the site and are talking to them on a daily basis.

However, there are other issues, like the hygiene issues especially due to lack of ablution facilities, water to take bath etc. Luckily, it was not a small confined space that they were trapped, but a 2-kilometer stretch.

There are many health issues that people who are trapped in dark closed spaces face:

- Respiratory infections, from mild to serious ones like pneumonia and tuberculosis
- Depression and psychosis due to fear of imminent death
- Behavioural changes due to absence of light
- Circadian rhythm which helps the body operate a healthy sleep-wake schedule may get affected leading to lack of energy, memory issues, problems with digestion and bowels
- PTSD (post trauma stress disorder) may be seen once they are rescued out
- Their pre-existing medical conditions can aggravate

What should have been done until they were rescued out:

- Get soft-spoken, mature and articulate doctors which should include Internists, Psychiatrists and Occupational Health physicians to talk to them, in addition to the local government doctors who have undoubtedly done a marvellous job

- Get popular sportspersons and film stars to interact with them, rather than India's Principal Secretary. This is because the worker doesn't know who or what a Principal Secretary is but they know a Dhoni or a Virat
- If the majority of workers are from a particular region, get popular persons from those geographies as they will relate will them and feel good and encouraged. Getting MS Dhoni and Rishabh Pant would have been even more useful
- Provide guided meditation to the trapped workers

What should be done once the workers are out:

- Talk encouraging words
- Do not overwhelm them by showing opulence
- Provide nutritious food for a few days to build up the lost body mass. This should be done in a government accommodation which has a spacious garden as it is good for mental health
- Relocate their families to stay with them for a few days
- Get physical examination as well as psychiatric evaluation
- Treat the PTSD (post-traumatic stress disorder), if any
- Provide paid leave for a few days to be with their families and some cash incentive

The members of the various rescue teams, especially the rat-hole miners, should also be appropriately taken care of by the government authorities and their work-related and other concerns addressed.

This is also the time government should consider to improve the working conditions of all workers proactively as they are an asset to any country and be aware that India has an expertise of around 3000 medical professionals who specialize in Occupational (work-related) Health and can assist the government formulate a plan to protect worker health across all industries.

The photographs of most of the workers once they were out were of joy, obviously. This demonstrates the natural resilience the Indian worker has; and I hope it will remain, so that they don't get into PTSD.

How many of these 41 workers will rejoin or do similar jobs will depend on how they are handled by the government authorities after they are rescued.

The Silkyara tunnel collapse reminds me of the Than Luang cave rescue in northern Thailand in June-July 2018. Twelve members of a junior football team aged 11 to 16, and their 25-year-old assistant coach got trapped in the cave on 23 June 2018 where they went after a practice session due to heavy rains that began soon after they entered.

On 2 July, British divers John Volanthen and Rick Stanton advanced through the narrow passages and muddy waters and found the group alive on an elevated rock about 4 kilometres (2.5 mi) from the mouth of the cave. Between 8 and 10 July, all 12 boys and their coach were rescued from the cave by an international team.

The coach had previously been a Buddhist monk, and had guided meditation for the children during the 18-day ordeal.

The rescue effort involved as many as 10,000 people, including more than 100 divers, scores of rescue workers, representatives from about 100 governmental agencies, 900 police officers, and 2,000 soldiers. Ten police helicopters, seven ambulances, more than 700 diving cylinders, and the pumping of more than one billion litres of water from the caves were required.

Highlighted below is how Elon Musk, a U.S businessman got involved in a similar crisis in 2018:

On 3 July 2018, a user on Twitter asked if Elon Musk could "assist in anyway to get the 12 Thailand boys and their coach out of the cave". The following day, Elon replied "I suspect that the Thai govt has this under control, but I'm happy to help if there is a way to do so". By 6 July, Elon commented that engineers for SpaceX and Boring Company would reach Thailand to see if they could assist the government in the rescue.

On 7 July, based on the feedback received from the cave experts in Thailand, Elon Musk, by the same evening, announced that construction on the submarine (light enough to be carried by two divers and small enough to fit through the narrow gaps) was complete and that it was on its way to Thailand.

On 8 July, Elon shared a video of the submarine being tested in a pool through a simulated narrow passage. By 9 July, Elon commented that the "mini-sub" was ready if needed and that it would be left in Thailand if they need it for the rescue or in the future.

By 10 July, all 12 boys and their coach were successfully rescued and the submarine was never used in the rescue but was left in Thailand for later use, if any.

The Elon Musk involvement demonstrates that we must escalate difficult issues to the highest possible expertise available on Earth and find solutions because every life is precious!

At the same time, never forget what Elbert Hubbard said, 'One machine can do the work of fifty ordinary men. No machine can do the work of on extraordinary man'. The rat-hole miners were extraordinary!

6

WHO launches a Commission to tackle loneliness

(published on 26th November, 2023 in www.occupationist.com)

On 15th November 2023, a news flashed out from the WHO (World Health Organization) headquarters announcing a new Commission on Social Connection to address loneliness, with US Surgeon General Dr Vivek Murthy as its co-chair.

In 2018, UK had appointed its first Minister for Loneliness.

"For too long, loneliness has existed behind the shadows, unseen and underappreciated, driving mental and physical illness," Dr Murthy said. "Now, we have an opportunity to change that."

In 2018, UK had appointed its first Minister for Loneliness. In 2021, Japan appointed its own Loneliness Minister as suicide rates increased for the first time in 11 years. In the first week of November 2023, New York state appointed sex therapist Dr Ruth Westheimer as its first loneliness ambassador.

Loneliness economy is growing - dating apps, robot pets, hugging apps etc. are all in the market. Sadly, they are band-aid approaches without addressing its root cause, and that's the fear - even if loneliness economy grows, loneliness may end up causing a dent in economies of nations!

The old corporate adage 'it is lonely at the top' is no more true! In fact, the C-suite executives and MSMEs (Micro Small Medium

Enterprises) business owners communicate with employees more often than before. Some even play golf and other sports with their employees.

Loneliness cuts across all ranks in societal hierarchy, continents, religion, age-groups, gender etc. It affects the rich and poor. Loneliness is omnipresent.

According to a global survey, 33% of adults globally feel lonely. Brazil tops the list with 50% of adults feeling lonely often, always or sometime. In India, 46% of adults felt lonely at least sometimes. The numbers are an estimate, and something that we cannot ignore. What we are seeing may be the tip of the iceberg.

Intermittent loneliness has not spared anyone and resilient people generally overcome it. Sometimes intermittent loneliness is by choice – you want to be with yourself for a while. It's your 'me-time.' It is the chronic loneliness, which is never by choice, and which is a slow, silent killer that needs to be addressed. Each individual is different and each person's loneliness has a different reason.

Loneliness is historical, although the modern literature dates it around the Industrial Revolution. In India, thousands of years ago, rishis (sages) would go to isolated places like the Himalayas to meditate. Rishis either just lived there or returned, giving path-breaking philosophies of life. All these sages went to remote places on their own; it was their choice.

Long-term loneliness by choice is solitude. In solitude, one chooses to disconnect from people for a purpose and this is because solitude is restorative and it provides the bandwidth to think, plan, recharge and create.

When intermittent loneliness is by choice, I called it aloneness. In aloneness, one is disconnected from people, by choice. Loneliness is usually destructive while aloneness is mostly meditative. Loneliness hurts while aloneness soothes.

> ***Loneliness is usually destructive while aloneness is mostly meditative.***

So, loneliness is nothing new; and, it was never an issue to be addressed as it was usually intermittent whether by choice or otherwise. Also, earlier we used to avoid talking about it. Today we are more vocal, thanks to social media. And the population of the world has increased; so, the number of lonely people has increased. The WHO (World Health Organization) has realized it and is addressing the issue.

The paradox of social media is that although it is supposed to connect people, yet it disconnects them, perhaps due to the physical distance (as there is no face-to-face interaction) and the differences of opinion that it creates. Meeting in person is seldom an element of social media which is how it creates the disconnect and becomes a contributor to loneliness.

It is important to remember that loneliness evolved as a survival tool and it reminds us of the significance of companionship, but becomes a silent killer when there is lack of companionship. The unpleasant feeling that loneliness creates encourages us to be connected with fellow human beings which assures our place in the group thereby increasing our chances of survival. Loneliness evolved and motivated humans to stay together in groups and improve chances of survival long enough to pass on the genes.

Historically, if you were alone, you would be eaten up by wild animals; hence there was the need to connect. For most part of human history, in the absence of connecting with fellow human beings, death was inevitable. Hence loneliness, if ever present, was never prolonged.

Today there are no wild animals, and so most people think that the need to be physically connected is less important. They are happy to be app-connected via WhatsApp, Facebook, LinkedIn, Instagram etc. It works for a short while - months or a few years. In the interim, after a few days or weeks, the mind wants to physically connect with people. If this want is suppressed due to whatever reasons, the person becomes alone and if unchecked enters the blackhole of loneliness. By this time, the interest in app-connection also diminishes as it no longer provides the excitement it earlier did.

To escape the blackhole state of loneliness, make every attempt to be physically connected in this app-connected world; and sooner the better. The world of blackhole state of loneliness is so deep, dark and dangerous that coming out of it is quite an effort once it is long-term or chronic. Parents, friends and relatives must be able to appreciate the features of loneliness and be able to reach out.

How to recognize loneliness in individuals:

- appear disconnected from other people
- don't talk to others as much as they did earlier
- sad appearance

A big mental health pandemic is to be expected in the near future as the current younger generation (Millennials, GenZ and even Alpha) as well as the older one are majorly app-connected. All of us have to make conscious efforts to meet people more often. Work From Home is also creating loneliness as all communication is virtual (online) without much face-to-face interaction.

Modern way of living has increased the risk of getting lonelier. I remember as a child in the 1970s, we could go to anyone's house without a prior appointment; not anymore. This is akin to what the aristocrats did in the past; they isolated themselves from the society on the basis of wealth and status and confined themselves to a life of loneliness.

Loneliness is a survival tool and reminds us of the significance of companionship, but becomes a silent killer when there is lack of companionship.

According to historians, loneliness began during the Industrial Revolution (around 1760 AD) in Europe when people left their homes and families to work in factories. In the new towns and cities that formed around the factories the communities became smaller thus marking a start of a permanent roadway to loneliness.

Mankind has not been able to prevent loneliness; however, early recognition and timely steps taken can lessen it and that does have a positive impact on physical and mental health. The effect of loneliness is not only on the worker but also on families, especially if they are living far away, and that is why it needs to be tackled aptly.

As time passed, even distance did not matter for loneliness to set in. Today one can experience loneliness even in the same household and circumstances leading to it must be identified and acted upon before loneliness in one or more house members becomes chronic and debilitating.

In the modern era, as social media overrides companionship, loneliness has ceased to be a survival kit; in fact, it is a deadly epidemic that kills prematurely and that has made WHO to announce a new Commission on Social Connection. Loneliness is a public health problem.

Dr Karen DeSalvo, a committee member of the WHO Commission on Social Connection, who is also the chief health officer at Google, said that when she was a clinician and when she was health commissioner of New Orleans, she learned firsthand that "great care matters, but it has to happen in a context" – and that includes social connection.

Chronic loneliness can also lead to poor physical health. It is two times more dangerous than being obese; it is similar to being an alcoholic or smoking 15 cigarettes daily. The risk of premature death in lonely people is around 25 percent. The risk of stroke is around 30 percent. Loneliness is also associated with 50 percent increase in dementia.

People who are lonely also have more unhealthy habits (smoking, drinking excess alcohol, sedentary lifestyle) that accelerate aging and many life-threatening diseases. Research has also shown that lack of social connection is linked with poor mental health and an increased risk of anxiety, depression, and suicide.

There are many reasons for loneliness - living alone, leaving home for education, start of college life, chronic health issues, loss of family member or friend, limited financial resources, lower level of education, having a physical disability etc.

What can be done to undo loneliness?

It is never too late. Join meaningful associations and clubs where you can do good for society while making friends and break the trend of living alone. According to historian Keith Snell, the trend of living alone is the most significant cause of loneliness. Living with the family or close friends helps convert the dread of loneliness to a magic of connection.

One can prevent loneliness by being mentally strong. Don't let circumstances deter you from doing your work and achieving what you want; however, be realistic. Overcome all your shortcoming. There are plenty of examples of men and women in history who overcame one and all of the reasons cited above for loneliness and moved forward.

Research has shown that individualistic nations (USA, Europe including UK) have high levels of loneliness compared to collectivist cultures (Japan, China, Brazil, India etc.). However, this is changing due to globalization, consumerism and travel making loneliness more widespread and universal, including in India.

Loneliness is not always negative. If it can be a health risk, it can also be a spur to action. In order to create great work, writers like Virginia Woolf and May Sarton have harnessed not just solitude, but the aching pain of loneliness. Loneliness, for them was a privilege, a luxury on which they thrived.

Many are lonely in a crowd. In today's modern world, touching someone may not always be politically correct and it can be blown out of proportion. Touch is important while dealing with a person who is lonely, just as other senses like smell, taste and even sound (remember the joy of a ringing doorbell during Covid). And we are afraid to touch, thereby foregoing an effort to address loneliness. Touch a fundamental human need, like food, water and house.

Loneliness is not always negative; for some it is a privilege, a luxury on which they thrive.

Workplace loneliness was growing even before the Covid pandemic. In future, Work From Home is likely to immensely contribute to loneliness. It is a slow process and will take time to manifest; hence it is good to work at least 2 days in office every week. It is important to know that loneliness can occur in every worker, young or old, and workplace wellness programs must account for this and many other variables. Loneliness can affect a previously top performing employee. Upskilling and training will not improve performance of a lonely and isolated employee, identifying its reasons will.

Recent research has also pointed that workers working with AI systems may be prone to be lonely and Occupational Health physicians and/or wellness managers must be mindful of this and include these workers too in company's wellness programs and social events.

Some of the things that help combat workplace loneliness are:

- Welcome a new employee and make them comfortable in the new environment
- Prioritize talking about the organization
- Encourage talking and participating in all activities
- Assign a mentor
- Have team lunches
- Have regular internal communication
- Include in decision making

For some loneliness is a choice, albeit momentarily, and they thrive on it. For those in whom loneliness isn't out of choice, it is a difficult living, and they need help, sooner the better. How we respond to loneliness, in others and ourselves, requires maturity, insight, understanding and pondering. Hope the collective wisdom of mankind will come to the rescue of loneliness!

Leaders, both political and business, must realize the seriousness of the issue of loneliness and invest in wellness programs that account for loneliness as it will protect physical and mental health of individuals as well as economies of nations.

Loneliness hurts, it is painful; it causes diseases, it causes premature deaths, it reduces worker performance and hence industrial productivity. Loneliness can be prevented or lessened and the people made happy and productive. Like the UK and Japan, all countries must appoint a Minister for Loneliness. India is no exception; it is time India appoints a Minister for Loneliness.

7

Is your office as safe for your health as it looks?

(published on 21st November, 2023 in www.occupationist.com)

Companies and some Occupational Health (OH) physicians often get overwhelmed when it comes to establishing OH in the factory and/or office. In India, companies usually comply by establishing OH in their factories as per recommendations of Indian Factories Act. However, there are companies who go far beyond the local laws.

Occupational Health is a medical specialty that is preventive. There are methods by which OH prevents hazards at workplace from harming employee health. OH identifies hazards and takes steps to mitigate them to as low as reasonably practicable so that employee health is preserved.

Most employers/companies lack an awareness and hence do not even consider that hazards could be present in their well-appointed, safe-looking corporate office. Look of an office may be pleasant to the eyes, it may not be pleasant to people occupying it, especially in the long run. An employee working in the office can be exposed to a lot of hazards that could harm health, depending on the job being done.

Office housekeeping is usually managed by the Admin team and they do a wonderful job in keeping the office clean. Inputs sought by the Admin team from a OH physician will bring synergy to the clean office and make the office safe too for employee health. A small office, or a large corporate office having thousands of employees may not be keen to establish OH as they are out of Indian Factories Act. Absence of OH in offices can harm employee health - we will see it in the paragraphs below.

A clean looking office should not be mistaken for a safe office. In fact, no workplace (office or factory) is safe for human health; it has to be made as safe as reasonably practicable.

Look of an office may be pleasant to the eyes, it may not be pleasant to people occupying it.

How to make an office safe?

Ideally, an Occupational Health Risk Assessment (OHRA), however basic, should be undertaken to identify all hazards in the office and steps taken to mitigate them. Even if OH is established in bits and pieces, it will help, rather than not taking any action about the potential hazards in the office.

By bits and pieces Occupational Health is meant that even if an office is unable to establish OH to a certain level due to lack of expertise or financials, taking up any of the hazards identified or doing a little bit randomly will at least take care of a hazard potentially harmful to health. Over a period of time, various hazards could be picked up for its mitigation to make the workplace safer.

Let us see a few of the many examples of hazards that are found in an office which can be unsafe for the health of the workers.

1. Working with computers: In offices, most of the employees work with computers. It is the time spent continuously with computers that causes harm to health in the form of headache, eye strain, wrist pain, numbness in fingers, neck pain, back pain etc.

There are a few ways by which employees can escape these health issues, the basic being taking frequent breaks. I suggest a break for 2 minutes after every 30 minutes and this is how the break has to be taken – stretch yourself while in the chair; then, rotate your eyeballs clockwise and anti-clockwise; after which, get up from the chair, walk a few steps, go near a window, see a distant object and return back to the chair. How many of us do that? A break like this will prevent aches and pain that a person working with computers can get at the end of the day.

Another approach is to do a workstation ergonomic assessment, which also can be done by installing a software in the computer. I have an experience of using Remedy and I found it immensely useful. After the assessment using Remedy, it prompts to instal a software in the computer that tracks how much time you have spent with the computer and other details, and based on this info it prompts you when to take a break, its various options and the duration of the break.

Last but not the least, make sure you drink enough water to manage fatigue that can set in due to work.

2. Food and water safety: If food is provided by the employer, it becomes a moral responsibility to provide safe and healthy food. In case of food poisoning, food supplied by the employer and consumed in its work locations is considered an Occupational (work-related) illness.

If food is not provided by the employer, there must be arrangements to keep the food safe that employees bring from home. A refrigerator, a microwave oven be provided by the employer for use by employees as necessary. Food stored to consumed later must also be at the right temperature.

Unsafe food leads to food poisoning that impacts many employees at the same time and hence it is necessary to be mindful of it and not lose day(s) due to ignoring a simple consideration.

3.Provision of first-aid: It is good to offer first-aid training to employees, have a tie-up with an ambulance provider and access to multi-specialty hospitals nearby, and if possible, to be able to manage illnesses or accidents that might occur in the office premises until expert help arrives.

4.Air-conditioning and air-quality: The temperatures in the offices must be properly maintained. We talk about air pollution but what about air-quality in the office areas? It is advisable to check the HVAC (Heating, Ventilation and Air Conditioning) control system and air quality once in 6 months or as necessary.

5.Storage: Pesticides, if at all should be stored separately, away from where food is stored. Handling of pesticides should be done only by personnel trained in it.

6.Changing room: Food-handlers and janitors must have designated changing rooms.

7.Training: Food-handlers and janitors should undergo regular training regarding personal hygiene. Supervisor managing food-handlers and janitors must follow a daily check-list and take timely action if deficiencies are found.

8.Unseen hazards: Discrimination, toxic culture, overwork, etc. are some of the unseen hazards at workplace that if not addressed aptly can lead to resentment, absence from work, attrition, low performances and eventually an illness. Wellness programs which are part of OH setup must account for these unseen hazards and any other, and address them effectively by having policies, including zero-tolerance as necessary.

9. Etc.

In addition, there is Sick Building Syndrome (SBS) and Building Related Illness (BRI), about which I will blog separately in future.

If the office does not have a doctor (either part-time or full-time), a Walkthrough Workplace Assessment (WWA) of workplace helps. WWA is done by a randomly picked team of office employees from various departments led by a member of a senior management or even a CEO, who walk around the office and look for safety and/or health hazards. WWA is useful even if you have a doctor or an OH physician as new hazards may crop up anytime.

In a workplace where there is a doctor (either OH physician or a doctor with interest in Occupational Health), the admin and the HR with the support of senior management can work together in sync with the doctor and seek health related inputs to provide a clean looking yet 'safe for health' workplace.

Even if Occupational Health is established in bits and pieces, it will help, rather than not taking any action about the potential hazards in the office.

The same applies to employees who work from home. In fact, employees those who work from home are in danger of deteriorating their health faster than office going employees – both physical health as well as mental health.

So, if you thought that office is a safe place and cannot harm your health, think again! Ditto for your home, if you are 'working from home' you could be harming your health too more than if you opt for 'hybrid mode of working' rather than any one. Safe practices observed in an office could be duplicated at home to protect not only your health but also of family members.

Establishing OH practices and involving the employees in workplace often brings rewards in terms of employee satisfaction; and is one of the ingredients in improving workplace productivity.

This is also the time for all stakeholders to act and make the workplace compliment your health and not rob away your energies by the end of the day or even during mid-day.

8

Discrimination at workplace and high blood pressure

(published on 15th November, 2023 in www.occupationist.com)

The world in general and workplaces in particular are becoming a difficult place to be. A recent study published in Journal of the American Heart Association (JAMA) in April 2023 seem to suggest that those who experienced workplace discrimination developed high blood pressure.

One of the risk factors for high blood pressure is discrimination at work.

"The daily hassles and indignities people experience from discrimination are a specific type of stress that is not always included in traditional measures of stress and adversity," says sociologist David R. Williams, professor of public health at the Harvard T.H. Chan School of Public Health.

The discrimination could be on the basis of race, religion, region, nationality, colour, gender, appearance – just about anything. All these creates a toxic workplace and the company policy should spell out very clearly about the actions that could be taken on employees who indulge in discrimination.

In a sample study of 1246 US workers, the researchers found that those who experienced discrimination on the job were 54% more likely to develop high blood pressure compared to those workers who had minimum exposure. The 2023 study published in JAMA is the first study to demonstrate that discrimination in the workplace can raise blood pressure.

Most of the participants were middle-aged, white, and married. They were mostly non-smokers, drank up to moderate amounts of alcohol, and did moderate or more exercise. No one had high blood pressure at the start of the study.

Employees who felt discriminated developed high blood pressure at a rate of about 4% each year compared to 2.5% per year in people who had minimum encounters to discrimination.

Lead researcher, Jian Li, professor at the University of California, Los Angeles said, "Our findings suggest workplace discrimination as a potential risk factor for high blood pressure."

The study followed workers for a long time, showing that the high blood pressure diagnosis was after they started to experience discrimination.

The researchers used the following 6 questions:

- How often were tasks given to you that no one else wanted to do
- How often are you under watch compared to fellow coworkers
- How often did your line manager use slurs (ethnic, racial, sexual) or jokes at you
- How often did your coworkers use slurs (ethnic, racial, sexual) or jokes at you
- How often did you feel ignored by your line manager
- How often did a coworker with lesser experience and/or qualification got a promotion before you

Discrimination leads to stress that activates body's fight-or-flight response which results in faster heart beats and narrowing of the blood vessels that causes a temporary rise blood pressure. If the stress response is triggered often, it can lead to blood pressure remaining high and requiring treatment.

Chronic stress reduces the ability of the body to recover from stressors. The ongoing stress may take a toll indirectly by making people to cope in unhealthy ways (smoking, drinking etc.), disrupting sleep and in the process making it difficult to have an exercise regime.

In the past studies have tried to establish a connection between chronic stress and physical health, however, recently research has started to focus on health effects of racism. And even less is known about discrimination at work.

Sickness at workplace not only affects one worker but all those who are doing similar jobs or encountering unpleasant work-related issues in the same location.

People should be aware that even words they consider "jokes" can have lasting effects on others, Sanchez, Chief Medical Officer for Prevention at American Heart Association said.

Depending on degree of workplace discrimination, the risk of developing high blood pressure increased accordingly.

The researchers had factored in many variables, such as age, race, income and education level, and exercise, smoking and drinking habits etc.

Dr Eduardo Sanchez, chief medical officer for prevention at the AHA (American Heart Association) said that given that people spend so much of their lives at work, it is very important to study the health effects of job exposures.

Not only high blood pressure, multiple studies in the past have documented that experiencing discrimination increases risk for developing a range of factors linked to heart disease, which also includes chronic low-grade inflammation, obesity, and type 2 diabetes.

The author of this article is of the view that health effects of job exposures must be studied not just in factories but in corporate offices too. Many business owners and even employees are often of the view that a corporate office is a safe place for health, but it isn't. In fact, no workplace is safe, it has to be made as safe as practically possible.

Analysing and addressing job exposures at workplace is not only good for the employees but for businesses too as healthy, happy employees are more productive than when sickness strikes.

In fact, discrimination at work is nothing new, in 1997 David Williams, Professor at Harvard TH Chan School of Public Health, created the ***Everyday Discrimination Scale*** which is the most widely used measure of effect of discrimination on health.

Sickness at workplace not only affects one worker but all those who are doing similar jobs or encountering unpleasant work-related issues in the same location. Hence work-related (occupational) health risk assessments (OHRA) are so useful and often the first important step to protect employee health.

One of the risk factors for high blood pressure is discrimination at work. Hence if discrimination is reported or felt by a group of employees in any organization, it must be immediately and appropriately addressed by the management. However, at the organizational level, no studies have directly addressed this issue.

Is there a role for the Occupational Health physicians who are doctor employed in the industry (either full-time or part-time)?

Yes, the Occupational Health physician employed in the industry does have a role as they deal with worker health. Just as fear of working with inadequate or poor safety systems at workplace can affect mental health, similarly, discrimination is a subtle yet powerful stressor that can affect health as noted in the above paragraphs.

> ***Many business owners and even employees are often of the view that a corporate office is a safe place for health, but it isn't.***

In fact, physicians in the industry may start asking leading questions about discrimination at work if they record high blood pressure in an employee as part of their examination. Based on this data, at an organizational level, it must be appropriately and immediately addressed as per company policy.

At a personal level, affected employees may be advised stress relieving methods like deep breathing, relaxation techniques, mindfulness, regular exercise, adequate sleep etc. to cope with the negative thoughts that often arise due to discrimination.

Affected employees should be advised to refrain from coping the effects due to discrimination by starting to or increasing to smoke, drink etc. as it is often counter-productive.

Lastly, as the world and the workplaces evolve in the next few years, the fear is about legal costs and reputational risks due to discrimination will increase. It's time the senior management in companies take the issue of discrimination at workplace urgently!

9

The 70-hour workweek: Should India work so much?

(published on 5th November, 2023 in www.occupationist.com)

Recently one of India's IT leader and Infosys founder NR Narayana Murthy, whom many including me hold in high esteem, sparked a debate when he spoke about working for 70-hours per week.

In the past, many Indian leaders have voiced similar views. Bhavish Aggarwal, CEO of Ola went on to say that it is 'our moment to go all in and build in one generation what other countries have built over many generations.'

Shantanu Deshpande, the CEO of Bombay Shaving Company, had said in a LinkedIn post that freshers should work 18 hours per day. 'Eat well and stay fit, but put in the 18-hour days for at least 4-5 years,' he said. Some sage advice but he was trolled in social media and eventually had to apologise and say that it was not meant to be taken literally.

Some global leaders also pitch for similar hours. Chinese businessman Jack Ma of Alibaba had the 996 rule, that is, work from 9 am to 9 pm 6 days a week. In China, Jack Ma was criticized by social media users saying that it will affect family life, and no one will have children because of lack of time.

Elon Musk, world's richest man and CEO of many companies including Twitter (now X) asked the Twitter staff to work more than 100 hours per week.

If the employee was hired at a 40-hour salary, companies will have to budget this in their expenditure because you can't demand a 70-hour week at a 40-hour salary.

Now, what is wrong in a 70-hour week or 12-hours day. Nothing really, if you are working for your own company or start-up, are working on a project that is for a few weeks and most importantly, if you enjoy the entire experience. Basically, if you have a sense of purpose, it won't harm or kill you prematurely. Death is a multi-factorial journey and work (both overwork and underwork) is just one of its reasons. However, both, overwork and underwork can have disastrous effect on mind and body, especially if it is against the wish of the employee and goes on for a long time, and any good work culture should account for that.

Those who want to work or have to work 70 hours or more are already doing so, routinely. For those who want to work it is a matter of choice, for those who have to work it is matter of survival.

Working 70 hours or more per week can't be a rule. It can be an exception though. We live in an orderly world – there is WHO (World Health Organization) and there is ILO (International Labour Organization). The work guidelines of these two global bodies must be respected.

Indian worker is already working 47.7 hours per week on an average, according to International Labour Organization (ILO) data updated in 2023. In a comparison of 10 big economies, Indians have the longest average work week. India ranks 7th in the global ranking with only Qatar, Congo, Lesotho, Bhutan, Gambia, and the United Arab Emirates averaging more, which is what makes the ILO prepare a special India-specific report on working hours.

Most workers will not be happy to work for 70 hours per week. This will lead to a lot of unhappiness, which in turn will lead to lot of diseases, low productivity and defeat the very idea of creating national wealth. The wealth created will be less due to low productivity and whatever wealth is produced will go into treating the diseases caused by unhappiness due to 70 hours workweek.

Meanwhile, a survey done in 2018 by Harvard Business Review said that CEOs in the US work 9.7 hours per weekday, and another 3.9 hours per weekend day, that is almost 53 hours per week. They also work during vacations. And they do it week after week till they are at the helm of affairs.

A one-day break taken by a CEO during a crisis can cost him/her the job as it happened during the Gulf of Mexico oil spill in 2010.

Another survey of 357 Indian CEOs of listed Indian manufacturing firms by International Growth Centre (economic research outfit) revealed that the average Indian CEO works 39 hours a week. This meant most CEOs work for close to 8 hours a weekday.

It is interesting to note that countries with shorter working hours have higher Per Capita GDP (see the table below):

Country	Average hours* worked/week	GDP (PPP**) in US $ per capita 2022
India	47.7	$ 8379
China	46.1	$ 21,476
South Korea	37.9	$ 50,070
Japan	36.6	$ 45,573
USA	36.4	$ 76,399
Netherlands	29.5	$ 49,979

Countries with shorter working hours have higher Per Capita GDP

*Source: ILO (International Labour Organization)

**PPP (Purchasing Power Parity) takes into account relative cost of living, rather than using only exchange rates, therefore providing a more accurate picture of real differences in income. Source: worldometers.info*

All this reminds me of two stories, one of Steve Jobs, a real character and another Tom Sawyer, a fictional one created by Mark Twain in 1876.

Tom Sawyer, an orphan boy full of mischief but pure-hearted, gets punished by Polly, his aunt because he angers her by eating jam and then getting into fight with another boy. The punishment is to whitewash the fence, an unpleasant task in his eyes. However, Tom gets a number of other boys to whitewash the fence by convincing them that whitewashing is fun. By making the work look extremely absorbing, Tom, an all-American boy not only gets the work of whitewashing the fence but the boys end up giving him various items for a turn at the fence.

On the other hand, Steve Jobs, founder of Apple and an all-American boy with an Indian philosophy influence, had once bragged to the press that the MacIntosh team was working 90 hours a week. Obviously, MacIntosh was Apple's first computer for mass consumption and so a lot had to be done. Steve would call his engineers on holidays and weekends because they felt the experience of working with him was worth it. The engineers could not resist working with Steve Jobs.

After being sacked from Apple, the company that Steve created, he returned to Apple in 1996 and worked from 7 am to 9 pm every day, since he was also leading Pixar (another company he created when he was sacked from Apple) operations. All those extended hours were put by Steve because Pixar was his company and he was passionate about work in general. No one told Steve Jobs to work extended hours; no one could tell him!

Only if managers and CEOs are like Tom or Steve will some of the employees voluntarily work more than ILO-scheduled 40 hours per week in case a time-bound project has to be completed. However, it cannot go on day after day endlessly.

Rather than hours, one should focus on quality of work, management techniques to get quality work done better and engineering methods to do quality work faster and cheaper. Cheaper, better, faster is the mantra of manufacturing.

Those who want to work or have to work 70 hours or more are already doing so, routinely. For those who want to work it is a matter of choice, for those who have to work it is matter of survival. To name a few of them – homemakers, working women managing homes, single parents, doctors, gig workers (a person who does temporary work, freelance work, or anyone engaged in an informal work on-demand basis or those who work on a part-time basis to earn supplementary income), migrant workers engaged in farming and construction, aspiring sportspersons, research scholars etc.

The statement by Narayana Murthy and the consequent debate about working hours is actually a good one as it raises questions about work, occupational (work-related) health, gender roles, and societal expectations. At a time when mental health is being recognized in India as a risk to be mitigated, and as India continues to evolve, it is necessary that the debate around workers, gender equality, work-related (occupational) health impacts and work-life balance continues and produces solutions that are doable for the employees in India.

As an Occupational Health physician, it would not be appropriate for me to advise either the management or the employees to work beyond ILO-stipulated 40-hours per week. This is because I see a risk in overwork and my role as a physician is to mitigate those risks rather than aggravate it or create new ones and then find solutions which wouldn't be any different than reducing work hours and a host of others due to indirect damages.

In my world, I would advocate a 9432 rule – work from 9 to 4, 3 days in a week in office, 2 days in a week work from anywhere which works out to 35 hours per week. Some countries already are working 35 hours or less and some corporates discourage emails after working hours. I am waiting for it to happen in India - the GenZ or Alpha might do it!

———————————

10

Occupational (Work-Related) health risks and sustainable energy transition

(published on 30th October, 2023 in www.occupationist.com)

The traditional oil and gas sector, now called as energy sector is witnessing major changes. Conventional energy sources like oil (petrol, diesel etc.) wood, charcoal etc. are being displaced by 'green energy' to mitigate the dangerous and often irreversible effects of conventional energy on climate change.

Due to the transition in the energy sector from conventional energy to sustainable energy, the existing big hazards may become fewer while new and smaller hazards may increase.

The concern is that conventional energy is a major determinant in climate change which in turn impacts health of workers and communities.

What will happen to work-related (occupational) risks in the energy sector due to the transition to green energy or sustainable energy?

Due to the transition in the energy sector, the existing big hazards may become fewer while new and smaller hazards may increase. Surveillance and research will indicate if the new hazards in future are insignificant or pose any more dangerous impacts on health than the existing hazards noticed in the conventional energy sector.

As of now, we hope energy transition will make life of workers and communities better. Currently, it has been documented that the conventional energy is causing a lot of harm to people and environment.

Climate change due to use of conventional energy threatens health, and the threat is increasing.

Climate change is being caused due to our dependence on the present energy technology which is inefficient.

The world is witnessing climate change that is already causing dangerous weather conditions such as heat waves, heavy rainfalls, floods, high-velocity winds etc. which have lots of implications on health.

Few of the noticeable implications of climate change on health are:

- Excessive heat on communities especially in vulnerable populations
- Work-related (occupational) heat risk for outdoor workers
- Drought due to long-term weather changes and consequent food insecurity
- Worsening of air pollution
- Reduced availability of potable water and its quality
- Increase in disease risk, including food and water-borne as well as vector-borne diseases
- Changing aero allergen patterns (due to pollen, fungi spores, insects, biological debris etc.)
- Forced migration of species, including humans
- Civil disruption in unstable governments and marginally stable societies leading to increase in poverty, mental ill-health, undernutrition, unemployment in healthcare, violence, conflict etc.

The above-mentioned problems due to climate change have to be reduced to a level that will be at least tolerable in future, and the only way it can be achieved is by moving quickly to a 'sustainable energy regime.'

SE (sustainable energy) regime is a time in future when businesses will be conducted in a different way without destabilizing global balance and resources for the future while ensuring continuity.

The world is witnessing climate change that is already causing dangerous weather conditions such as heat waves, heavy rainfalls, floods, high-velocity winds etc. which have lots of implications on health.

Rio +25 'The Earth Summit' was an international conference held in Rio de Janeiro, Brazil to assess progress in achieving sustainable development and mitigating climate change, 25 years after signing of the UN Framework Convention on Climate Change.

Rene Mendes, Tee Guidotti, and their colleagues in 2012 conducted a study on the occupational health risks of specific alternative energy technologies for the World Health Organization to support development of a background briefing paper for the Rio +25 summit.

The goal of this study was to anticipate the consequences of sustainable energy technology for occupational health and safety and the hazards or risks they may present. The purpose was to find if avoidable risks for workers could be reduced, to identify opportunities for making gains in the health of workers, their families, and the communities.

It is important for all business owners to realize that sustainability is an ethic issue, a business strategy and a social movement and that there is nothing intrinsically safer in SE compared to conventional energy technologies and both are equally harmful.

The study found that in general that technologies used in sustainable energy share the risks with other projects of similar scale and are the same as for conventional technology. The principles of hazard control and ensuring safe working conditions do not change.

In this context, a word about Tesla (a Elon Musk's company) controversy and how it continues to lead US carmakers in safety violations is warranted. Since 1st March 2019 when Forbes magazine reported that Tesla has been fined more times than 14 other car manufacturers combined in US with violations and fines under OSHA (Occupational Safety and Health Administration) rules.

However, Tesla, like other car manufacturers, has tried to maximize employee health with programs like stretching to reduce strain, have athletic trainers and massage tables for assembly workers. Occupational Health practices seem to be in bits in pieces.

In May 2022, Elon Musk said at the *All In Summit* in Miami, 'Tesla is sort of pretty far out there in terms of work ethic anywhere in the world.' The Tesla work ethic in the US, I think, is substantially greater than any other car company or any large manufacturing company that I'm aware of.', he said.

The Tesla story is for us to understand that it is important for all business owners to realize that sustainability is an ethic issue, a business strategy and a social movement. Since sustainability is perceived to be committed to health for all, employers in SE technologies are held to a higher standard because of their engagement in social equity and social expectation. There is nothing intrinsically safer in SE compared to conventional energy technologies and both are equally harmful.

The study found that in general that technologies used in sustainable energy share the risks with other projects of similar scale and are the same as for conventional technology. The principles of hazard control and ensuring safe working conditions do not change.

Sustainable development must be able to provide for healthy, safe and decent jobs in the new economy based on renewable energy. Workers should get the benefits of the transition as they are part of the community as well as key agents of change (builders of new sustainable energy economy) and should be protected from any adverse effects arising out of work.

Occupational Health plays an important role in sustainability as the basic principles of sustainability are similar. Protecting worker health is as much a part of sustainability as managing HSE and any other corporate responsibility, and is even more embedded in the values of sustainable development.

Hence research, surveillance and good practices of occupational health should continue to check if SE technology causes harm to human health, health of other species and the environment even though current research says sustainable energy does not pose any greater problem than conventional energy for worker health.

Work-Life Balance: An ingredient to make better managers

(published on 21st November, 2023 in www.occupationist.com)

Recent research has indicated that having a work-life balance in your daily regime may make you a better manager. Isn't it something to pursue? Is there a role for an Occupational Health physician here?

Occupational Health (OH) as a medical specialty is evolving and hence roles of the OH physicians are expanding compared to what they did in industries and offices, say, about a decade ago.

When everyone today is talking about work-life balance (WLB), few know about one of its side-effects. If WLB is incorporated in daily regime, its side-effects are manifold, one of which is that WLB can make its practitioner a better manager.

In many corporations, OH physicians manage the wellness agenda that includes work-life balance. However, until this research was out, no one knew if talks, workshops etc. on WLB were contributing in making better managers. In organizations having a WLB support by the management, better managers were being made as a side-effect of WLB advocacy. It was all happening unknowingly.

At the same time, it was also a HR initiative to make better managers via different types of trainings. WLB was being considered during such trainings but merely as a passing reference.

Work-life balance can make its practitioner a better person and a better manager.

Based on this research, a stronger advocacy regarding WLB in organizations is necessary. At the same time, it is imperative for both the OH physician and the HR to effectively promote WLB as it may make better managers and hence better organizations. The OH physician is well-versed to provide inputs on WLB to make the ongoing HR-led trainings for managers more effective.

This research which was published in *Journal of Applied Psychology*, found that seniors who shut off their emails as well as calls and job-related stress after work hours were successful in developing younger employees achieve their goals and were viewed by them as better managers.

The lead author of the research Klodiana Lanaj said, "We found that when leaders psychologically detached from work when at home -- they did not actively think about work-related issues, but instead engaged in activities that allowed them to disconnect and recharge – they felt more energized the next day at work, in ways that made them more effective as rated by their direct reports."

Managers who were able to compartmentalize between life at work vs life at home ended up "rated as more transformational and powerful by their subordinates," said Lanaj, an associate professor of management at the University of Florida Warrington College of Business.

"In contrast, on days when leaders kept ruminating about negative aspects of their work while at home, they felt more drained the next day at work, and were less transformational and powerful," Lanaj added.

In 2019 Lanaj and her colleagues surveyed 73 full-time work managers/leaders, including human resources managers, directors of finance, general managers and/or chief engineers, with 60 percent being women.

The average time participants had been on the job was around eight years with each team having an average of nine employees.

The surveys were conducted for about an hour a day over 10 consecutive workdays, and it assessed the degree to which each team leader felt able to mentally detach when the work day ended.

Questions asked to the managers included how much their jobs affected them emotionally outside work hours, their energy levels at work, about their sleep time and quality, and about feeling of their own self, their competence, and leadership skills.

The 63 men and women who worked for the managers were also surveyed by the research team.

To complete the research the team mates were asked how well the manager communicated goals and vision, displayed energy and enthusiasm, and/or challenged their team.

The team mates then rated the effectiveness of their managers.

In reality, modern work culture demands employees remain connected to work 24/7, literally, and this can seep energy of the team and the organization in the long run leading to work inefficiencies which can sometimes be gross. This research tells you exactly not to do that.

To de-stress, simple steps help, like, coming home in time, avoiding work-related activities at home, being with nature (having some plants or a fish tank), exercising regularly and spending time with family and friends.

Managers who work hard may improve their well being and hence be better managers by picking up a hobby as well as de-stressing using simple methods enumerated in the previous paragraph.

Incorporating Work Life Balance in one's life has many advantages – one of which is making of a better human being and hence a better manager. Better managers make better teams and better teams make better organizations!

Making work less stressful and making conscious efforts to reduce stress when not in workplace may be the first step to be a better manager, and it is something doable.

The outcomes of research like this may not be known to the HR manager or the senior management in an organization. However, if the organization employs Occupational Health (OH) physician(s) who are generally aware of such research should talk to the management and implement the findings to help an organization have even better managers.

This research and similar others indicate how an organization can have even better managers. The management has lot of challenges, one of being how to manage the Zoomers (GenZ) currently in workplace, and in future the Alpha generation who would join the workforce in 2032. The HR managers and senior management should be aware of these impending realities and prepare themselves seeking advice from various experts including the OH physicians.

Most of us do have some WLB in place but the need is to enhance it to be better persons as well as better managers. Now we have research to back the claims that makes better managers and hence organizations must pursue promoting WLB.

Incorporating WLB in one's life has many advantages – one of which is making of a better human being and hence a better manager. Better managers make better teams and better teams make better organizations!

12

Food and Water safety at workplace

(published on 15th October, 2023 in www.occupationist.com)

It is a moral responsibility of the food provider in case people get sick due to eating unsafe food provided by the food provider. It is an Occupational Illness (OI) if the food provided by the employer leads to sickness in the employees.

Food safety is important because unsafe food even now kills as per WHO estimate, about 4,20,000 every year globally and sickens around 600 million people despite the fact that more than 150 years ago, in 1862 President Abraham Lincoln had formed the USDA (United States Dept of Agriculture) and its Dept of Chemistry that eventually became FDA (Food and Drug Administration).

Human beings eat in large gatherings like workplace and functions (like marriages, conferences, seminars etc.), remote oilfields, aeroplanes etc. Each one of these places have hundreds of people and a 'bad' food can create havoc, chaos, hospitalizations, sickness absence, productivity losses, deaths, reputational issues etc.

In India, FSSAI (Food Safety and Standards Authority of India) was established on 5th September 2008 under Food Safety and Standards Act, 2006.

It is a moral responsibility of the food provider in case people get sick due to eating unsafe food provided by the food

provider. It is an Occupational Illness (OI) if the food provided by the employer leads to sickness in the employees.

Food poisoning has not spared anyone. It is said that Alexander the Great died of food poisoning, Mozart died of trichinosis (round worm infestation) and a US President Zachary Taylor died on 9th July 1850 of an 'unknown digestive ailment' potentially caused by eating raw fruit and drinking iced milk at a US Independence Day event on 4th July.

After the death of US President Zachary Taylor in 1850, it took America 12 years to form the FDA in 1862 under the Presidentship of Abraham Lincoln.

The Centers for Disease Control and Prevention (CDC) began keeping records on foodborne illnesses from 1970 onwards.

75 million cans of mushrooms from stores in USA were removed in 1973 after a country-wide outbreak of botulism.

In 1975, one of the worst food poisoning incidents happened when almost 200 people onboard a Japan Air Lines flight got severely sick after eating airline food.

Again in 1975, Lancet, a medical journal reported a study when more than half the passengers onboard a 3rd February 1975, flight from Anchorage, Alaska, to Copenhagen, Denmark, suffered a gastrointestinal illness with symptoms of nausea, vomiting, abdominal cramps, and diarrhea.

Perhaps due to these two horrific incidents airline food safety became very stringent. In Mumbai I have seen a huge food facility that manufactures food for multiple airlines as also for Presidents and Prime Ministers.

I have had the experience of managing two food poisoning incidents in the oilfields of Oman involving around 70-80 people each time. Luckily, most had mild symptoms and only 2-3 employees had to be transferred to a hospital. But the thought of managing 70-80 people in a remote location can be daunting. The incidents happened despite having a stringent food and water safety program. The possible cause was inability to maintain the temperature of cold foods due to extreme outdoor temperatures. In fact, most investigations of food poisoning in airlines that keep happening is due to outdoor temperatures being high as most of such incidents happen when food is picked up by airlines in Asia or Africa.

Most cases of food poisoning occur due to bacterial contamination (Salmonella, Staphylococcus, Vibrio etc.) but history is rife with chemical contamination leading to food poisoning. Chemicals do cause food poisoning.

Example: In 1955, in Morinaga Milk Industry in Japan, an industrial grade monosodium phosphate which contained an impurity of 5-8% arsenic, was added by mistake to milk produced by the company. Many babies were poisoned as the milk powder was used to feed them. More than 13,000 fell ill. By 1981 there were still more than 6000 people affected as adults with severe mental retardation and other health issues. And by 2006, more than 600 adults remained affected. A total of more than 600 people died due to this contamination.

Arsenic is a notorious chemical contaminant in foods. In the early 20th century, food poisoning was a major killer. England in 1900 witnessed the infamous English beer poisoning which affected more than 6000 people, leaving around 70 dead. Arsenic was introduced into the beer via contaminated sugar. The outbreak was made worse due to misdiagnosis of the illness.

A 'bad' food can create havoc, chaos, hospitalizations, sickness absence, productivity losses, deaths, reputational issues etc.

If in doubt, throw it out should be the mantra when it comes to dealing with food. It is so true, else bad food can lead to untold miseries due to something that could have been prevented.

Details about food safety is not within the scope of this blog, but suffice to say that efforts must be taken to make sure food provided by the employer (if providing food to workers) and the food manufacturer follows some basics as below:

- Location: The surroundings of the place of food manufacturing facility must be clean. It cannot be next to a garbage collection area or an open gutter.
- Raw material: Procure raw materials to prepare food from a reputed vendor. Inspect the vendor periodically, even if reputed.
- HACCP (Hazard Analysis Critical Control Point): Ensure its implementation if food is procured externally
- Refrigeration:
  - raw food
  - cooked food
  - veg food in upper trays, non-veg in lower trays
- Linear flow: In the kitchen it is about maintaining an order to cook a food item starting from storage, washing, cutting, mixing, cooking, cooling, packing and finally despatching.
- Food temperatures:
  - Cold foods: store, transport and serve below 5 degrees C
  - Hot foods: store, transport and serve around 65 degrees C
- Food-handlers:
  - Medical checks as per FSSAI recommendations (in India)
  - Training

- ➢ Handwashing
- ➢ How to receive food
- ➢ In house washing of utensils
- ➢ Well-fitted clothes
- ➢ Lifting techniques
- ➢ No use of jewellery

- Others:
  - Changing room: Industrial kitchen should have changing rooms for food-handlers to change before starting to prepare food
  - Washroom: Should be away from food storage, cooking areas with soap and air hand dryer.
  - Transportation of food: Use of insulated box keeps food dust-free and at requisite temperatures during transportation.
  - MERP: In large corporations or remote locations have a Medical Emergency Response Plan (MERP) to manage food poisoning, if ever it occurs.
  - Receiving cooked food from external contractor: Assign roles of responsibilities (Catering contractor, Employees, Admin, Health, Senior management etc.)
  - Engage the catering contractor: Feedback
  - Surprise inspections: Keeps the kitchen on their toes
  - Audits: Necessary for improvements
  - Documentation: Ensure accurate and complete documentation of all activities connected with food safety

The above basic steps are indicative. They give the reader an idea about the various steps to consider to make food safe, in homes, at workplace and in food manufacturing facilities. Small offices or workplaces may provide a microwave oven and a refrigerator for use by employees to heat and store food brought from home.

A detailed understanding on prevention of food poisoning can be had by a food expert or by contacting the author.

The role of OH physician is to support the admin to choose the right food supplier and maintain standards as one bad food experience at workplace leading to food poisoning can create a reputational issue for the employer.

13

Domestic Workers and Occupational Health

(published on 9th October, 2023 in www.occupationist.com)

Domestic work is an old occupation with ancient Mesopotamian (*present day Iraq, parts of present-day Iran, Syria, Turkey and Kuwait*) sources referring to it. Historically, domestic workers were employed by those who could afford a helping hand to do their daily chores.

Domestic work was and is a highly feminized unorganized sector with minimal to nil government regulations in most countries. They are informal workers who are not taken seriously – both by their employers and by themselves as a house is not even seen as a place of work. As a result, workplace hazards at homes get ignored and illnesses due to this occupation goes unanswered thereby adding to the global disease burden.

Like any other workplace, working in a home is not a safe place – it has to be made as safe as possible.

The incomes of a domestic worker are low compared to the intensity of their workload; women being paid lesser than men. This in turn means poor nutrition, limited access to healthcare in case of any illness/discomfort due to work.

What ails domestic workers globally despite the fact that they are so essential to a family is a matter of concern, as they are least respected, least paid, least rested (weekly offs and holidays), least supported in case of a health issue and most abused. They have no pension benefits, at least in developing countries. I think it is lack of awareness in people those who employ the domestic help as well as the domestic workers themselves.

In modern times, when both spouses are working, taking care of a domestic help should be a priority; sadly, it isn't. Priority because when both spouses go to work, it is the domestic help who takes care of the children and elderly at home. However, it is an observation that they are replaced if they ask for a raise or some benefits.

People often wonder what health issues can a domestic workers get due to working in homes. The people who employ them think home is the safest place to work, but alas, no, it is not.

Domestic work was and is a highly feminized unorganized sector with minimal to nil government regulations in most countries.

Like any other workplace, working in a home is not a safe place – it has to be made as safe as possible. And we are not talking here about the dangerous carbon monoxide emissions that can be found in homes, but simpler hazards on which action can be taken by the home owner themselves.

Example: Fumes due to cooking in the kitchen not able to find a way out from the window can cause breathing difficulty. All it needs is an exhaust fan to reduce the fumes. This will benefit both the domestic help as well as the home owner in case the necessity arises for them to work in the kitchen.

Anyone who does any work in a home, be it the owner or a domestic help is exposed to hazards. For example, a broom to clean the floor creates dust cloud that can cause allergic rhinitis; a cheap cleaning soap can cause allergic skin rash or eczema; lifting heavy weights can cause musculoskeletal issues, working without breaks can cause fatigue, lack of proper nutrition can cause fainting attacks etc.

Giving proper implements and materials is also important to prevent work-related health issues in a domestic help.

The house owner may not be able to systematically list all the hazards and take actions proactively but being aware and listening to feedback of domestic help and taking action can go a long way in preventing illness due to work as well as fostering a healthy and trusting working relationship. This is akin to what Ratan Tata did in the Indica car factory in the 1990s.

Ratan Tata had noticed the operators fix the rear strut of the car manually and would have to bend down 600 times to complete this operation on 300 cars each day. He had called his managers and asked, 'how can we expect our men to do this throughout their lives? Surely it will damage their health. We must provide an automation solution on priority.' The engineering department rose to the occasion and quickly developed a fixture to semi-automate the operation.

Ratan Tata became aware of the problem of the workers in the Indica car factory; he demonstrated compassion by seeing the suffering of the workers and its effect on their health and took action by asking the engineers to provide automation on priority.

Taking care of basic requirements of a domestic help and ensuring his or her health is preserved should be a priority, as it is useful to the house owner. An annual health check for the domestic help is useful. A sick domestic help can spread diseases, including tuberculosis.

Providing proper implements and materials is also important to prevent work-related health issues in a domestic help.

Domestic workers usually work alone; there is no support of co-workers or any protection from the law – all these makes them vulnerable to a lot of occupational illnesses that go unreported and wrongly treated. The treatment should have been to identify what is causing the illness and mitigating those causative factors, most of it could be done by the domestic worker and the employer. What happens on the contrary is the complaints of the domestic worker are being treated without mitigating the cause, in turn, sometimes creating another illness. That is why it is important to always consider '*is my sickness because of the work I do.*'

Bigger offices or factories employ a bigger number of workers who work similar to domestic help but with more clearly defined roles, weekly offs, salaries, medical checks, bonus etc. For example, there is food handler, cleaning staff, janitor etc. in large offices or factories. Proper training, equipment, materials are provided. The Admin or HR usually works closely with them and like any other employee, work-related health issues in them are proactively managed by the OH physician as also any new health issue.

Example: In one corporate office where I worked (which had just started), I noticed the housekeeping staff finding it difficult to shift large containers that would come periodically to the office. Immediately a trolley was ordered for them and 'lifting technique' was taught to them. Actions like these prevent any future musculoskeletal issues in them. All hazards in the office were identified and mitigated.

In homes, on the other hand, one domestic help usually does almost everything, one after the other – there is no rest period, no meals, no weekly offs, erratic salaries etc. That is why domestic workers are prone to more work-related illnesses and an early morbidity making them jobless much earlier.

When the home owner or the business owner speaks kindly to them, it makes a lot of difference to the morale of such workers. I recollect how even aircraft fueling attendants in the airstrips of oilfields of Oman would even walk up to the MD or the Dy. MD of the company (Petroleum Development Oman) as they alighted from the small aircrafts and shook hands and exchanged compliments with them. It makes world a wonderful place and workplace harmonious as opposed to 'toxic' if mutual respect is missing.

On the other hand I have heard from domestic helps how home owners treat them – they provide low quality cleaning agents that cause skin rashes, ask them to use underclothes as mops to clean the floor, do not provide them meals or even water, pay them lower than market rates, do not give them weekly offs, restricted long holidays, cut salary in case of sickness absence, sack them before it is Diwali (a major festival in India) so that they don't have to pay the bonus.

Do you think the above conditions are good for any worker? How can a worker be happy? Never create a situation where a worker can retaliate. Be polite, treat them nice and see the returns.

I know people who have one domestic help working with them for 35 years and the other for 21 years. They do their medical checks, once in two years. The domestic help have the house keys, and have even helped raise their kids. In return they have educated the children of their domestic help. They have plans to give a small pension for life. And most importantly, they respect them. Do what you can – if not monetary help, the least one can do is to treat them as another human being. It is good for their mental health too.

Make the work of domestic helps working for your home or office or a large organization safe, respectful, relaxed, and interesting to win their loyalty to get optimal results.

The ILO (International Labor Organization) has a Decent Work Agenda that encompasses most of the things discussed above.

———————————————

14

Breaks while working: Good for health, wellbeing, performance, and safety

(published on 9th October, 2023 in www.occupationist.com)

Actually, most of know taking breaks during working hours is good, without knowing why. Yet, we don't take breaks – again we don't know why. Taking breaks is important and equally important is to know why, where, when and how to take those breaks. The onus of encouraging employees to take breaks depends on the awareness and the approach of an organization's management and the role its managers play.

Anytime is a good time for a responsible break!

Awareness about significance of taking breaks is created by either HR or by a doctor (especially an Occupational Health physician) if the organization employs one. I remember once when I was working with an MNC, the participants were allowed to stand and listen to a speaker if sitting for a long time caused them discomfort. This was after an understanding with the CEO that it will improve attention of the employees. The presentation time of the speakers was reduced, and more bio-breaks were introduced – it is as easy as that.

Employees were happy with this initiative – the freedom to change postures when in discomfort. It was like taking a break, voiced many.

Taking breaks is important and equally important is to know why, where, when and how to take those breaks.

Taking frequent breaks throughout the day, including during non-work hours improves health, wellbeing, performance, and even safety.

Being productive is not about working for long hours, continuously. Many workers believe that spending more time on a job is equal to getting more done. In the long run that may not always be true. Workers skip lunch, stay after work hours and even avoid taking breaks for various reasons.

The onus of encouraging employees to take breaks depends on the awareness and the approach of an organization's management and the role its managers play.

Eventually such workers' pay a price as a recent survey from Aflac showed 59% of employees reporting feeling burnout. Add to this, employee engagement is declining among US workers (and must be declining elsewhere as well). Both, increasing burnout and reduced employee engagement are associated with hindered performance.

To address the issue of increasing burnout and declining employee engagement, the Harvard Business Review (HBR) team conducted a review of existing research on workplace breaks and analysed 80 studies. The team confirmed that stopping work for a short while throughout the day can improve wellbeing as well as help getting more work done. The research suggested that taking breaks within work hours does not reduce performance, in fact, it helps improve it.

Factoring reasonable work breaks can make the individual and/or the team more productive than trying to skip lunches and staying late at workplace. It disturbs work-life balance which in turn further reduces performance.

Taking work breaks is a very basic idea and small business owners should be aware of this if they want to improve their business performance and competitiveness. Encouraging their employees to take responsible breaks is better than not allowing them to take a break within work hours, as is the norm in small businesses.

Allowance of an even small break during work is a giant step in improving health, wellbeing, performance and safety of a worker.

However, the research pointed that not all work breaks are equally effective in improving wellbeing and performance. To make taking breaks effective, the following considerations are useful:

- **Length of the break:** Small frequent breaks (micro-breaks) for a few minutes help in improving performance and preventing fatigue. Breaks generally include getting off the chair, eating something, stretching or seeing a distant object from a window.
- **Timing of the break:** In the mornings, shorter breaks are useful. Longer breaks are effective in the second half of the work day (afternoon) as fatigue sets in and takes longer time to stabilise.
- **Where should the break be taken:** One can take a break sitting at the desk but research indicated that outdoor breaks were most effective especially in a green lawn.
- **Activities to be done during a break:** One should do some physical activity during the break – walk, stretch etc. to yield benefits of break time. If during a break you spend time on social media (and 97% of people do that), it leads to emotional exhaustion which reduces creativity as well as performance.

- **Role of pets:** Interactions with pets (a dog) helps but it may not be practicable in offices. However, I have advocated having a few small fish tanks in offices as they too have substantial benefits, are affordable and do not occupy much space.

What organizations can do to encourage breaks during work time:

- **Walk the talk:** The CEO and the senior management should 'walk the talk,' they should be seen taking breaks. In fact, the organization should have 'taking breaks' as one of the priorities to improve creativity and performance. In townhalls (employee gatherings), the CEO must emphasize on benefits of taking breaks, only then employees perceive it as a sanctioned benefit.
- **Have dedicated time for breaks:** It may not be possible in a big office employing thousands of employees, but teams could meet at a scheduled time for a short break once or twice a week, as in addition to fostering positive attitude towards breaks, it also helps bond the teams. On other days, to each one his/her own, one could take multiple breaks anytime.
- **List places for breaks:** The employees could go to a nearby green space (garden), or to a mall, or to a tea-stall (called tapri in India) depending on the location and size of its office. A large office complex that runs into acres may have everything inhouse and employees should be encouraged to make use of it.

Taking breaks during work time may be abused, hence the term 'taking responsible breaks' is apt and should be emphasized. Monitoring or doubting the employees 'break time' will not help – in fact, it will only increase the stigma and guilt that is prevalent around taking breaks, a reason why employees don't take breaks.

Individuals working in small businesses should talk to business owners and get a sanction to take responsible breaks, citing the Harvard Business Review study.

While organizations are redefining the issue of employee wellbeing, work break appears to be a promising tool to improve both – employee wellbeing as well as performance. The Occupational Health physician or the wellness manager, as the case may be, should make the senior management understand the value of research on work breaks so that they can encourage to design the process.

While the focus of this blog was on how work breaks can improve wellbeing and performance, it can be easily understood that taking frequent breaks also helps reduce the aches and pains due to repetitive tasks such as typing while working on computers etc. thus preventing employee health from deteriorating.

Breaks during work time are not only good for health, wellbeing and performance but also good for safety as they reduce fatigue and may prevent many accidents (industrial as well as non-industrial) that happen due to continuous working.

Individuals working in small businesses should talk to business owners and get a sanction to take responsible breaks, citing the HBR study as above. With time the business owners will realize that allowance of breaks has indeed helped improve business performance; with additional improvements in employee health (fewer sickness absence), happy employees (wellbeing) and employees who work safely (as they don't fatigue).

Allowance of an even small break during work is a giant step in improving health, wellbeing, performance and safety of a worker. Anytime is a good time for a responsible break!

15

AI Systems at workplace: An emerging concern in worker health

(published on 24th September, 2023 in www.occupationist.com)

It is not for the first time in modern history that workers are worried that machines or a new technology will render them obsolete and outdated. However, it is for the first time that research is being done aptly to know if a new technology or method of working (startups, work from home, gig economy) will have any impact on health.

Working with AI systems may disrupt health in future like never imagined, and everyone concerned with worker health and wellness must be aware of these.

Mechanization has been controversial since the start of Industrial Revolution (around 1720 AD). Machines improved productivity and raised incomes, but the workers perceived it as a threat to make them jobless, to lower their wages and to divert all the gains from growth to the owners of businesses. All these factors led the stocking-frame operators of Nottingham, UK (the Luddites) to damage the improved knitting machines that threatened their jobs. The workers also burnt the first mills that housed spinning and weaving equipment in the 1760s.

It is also important to remember that a technological change affects future of different trades differently.

Today, the workers don't destroy industries, instead they ask for their dues, few of them being – health care in general and specifically health protection due to the work they perform. Most business owners are considerate to their dues. It is only in the unorganized industries that workers are treated unfairly – and here both business owners and governments should act appropriately to avoid any major disruptions in work in future.

It is also important to remember that a technological change affects future of different trades differently. For example, In 1820, during the Industrial Revolution, the future of work for the wife of a farm laborer in England was not a happy one. This is because with the advent of spinning looms she had lost the opportunity to increase her family's income by spinning part-time, like her mother had done. The same was the fate of a farmer's wife in the deltas of Ganges (river Ganga) in India.

Recent research has found that people working with AI systems can develop insomnia, feel lonely, or even drink excessively after work.

However, some British women got to work in the cotton mills and these were more than that had been employed to spin cotton by hand. And during the same time, the future of work was bright for some trades – railway engineers, bricklayers, metal workers, etc. Also, a large number of middle-class entrepreneurs and professionals found huge success as they led the industrial economy.

Lately, there is a talk about AI (artificial intelligence) taking away jobs. That may be a bit premature – and instead of asking how AI will affect work or workers in future, one should ask what did the invention of the textile mill mean for a girl growing up in Manchester, UK, in 1800 or the wife of a poor rice farmer in the deltas of Ganges (river Ganga) in India at the same time. A new technology, AI for example, will affect futures of work very differently and often detrimentally. Something that we are witnessing now.

With this background, in this article, we will discuss if AI is affecting the health of the worker and how.

Recent research has found that people working with AI systems can develop insomnia, feel lonely, or even drink excessively after work.

The study that was published online on June 12 in the *Journal of Applied Psychology,* noted that these findings do not prove that working with AI systems causes loneliness or other responses; it is just that they are associated.

A new technology, AI for example, will affect futures of work very differently and often detrimentally. Something that we are witnessing now.

"The rapid advancement in AI systems is sparking a new industrial revolution that is reshaping the workplace with many benefits but also some uncharted dangers, including potentially damaging mental and physical impacts for employees," said lead researcher Pok Man Tang, an assistant professor of management at the University of Georgia.

"Humans are social animals, and isolating work with AI systems may have damaging spillover effects into employees' personal lives," Tang said in a journal news release.

The researchers found that working with AI systems can have some benefits too. For example, employees who use AI systems are more likely to be helpful to fellow workers, but this could be due to loneliness and the need for social outlet, Tang's team said.

Those who felt insecure and worried about social connections (attachment anxiety), reported that working with AI systems made them more likely to help others. This is because they suffered from loneliness and insomnia.

In an experiment, 166 engineers at a Taiwanese company working with AI systems were asked about their feelings of loneliness, attachment anxiety and sense of belonging. Those who worked more often with AI systems were more likely to experience loneliness, insomnia and increased after-work alcohol consumption. These workers also showed helping behaviours toward fellow workers.

Similar experiments in USA, Indonesia etc. pointed towards similar findings.

Tang was of the view that developers of AI should consider equipping AI systems with social features, such as a human voice, to mimic human-like interactions. Employers also could limit the frequency and duration of work with AI systems and offer opportunities for employees to socialize.

Working with AI systems may disrupt health in future like never imagined, and everyone concerned with worker health and wellness must be aware of these. Medico-legal cases may rise.

"Mindfulness programs and other positive interventions also might help relieve loneliness," Tang said. "AI will keep expanding, so we need to act now to lessen the potentially damaging effects for people who work with these systems."

As these are emerging concerns in worker health led by initial research, Occupational Health physicians employed in industries must have access to information regarding extent of use of AI systems or for that matter, any new technology or method of working.

When an Occupational Health (OH) physician identifies and reports that a worker working with AI systems is exhibiting loneliness or complaining of insomnia, the management must take steps as mentioned above to mitigate it. Taking timely steps may prevent many more workers working with AI systems in future to escape loneliness, insomnia or other serious health issues.

A lot of startups have workers who work with AI systems – startup owners must be aware of the possibility of AI systems affecting worker health and seek appropriate advice or take steps as mentioned above to mitigate it.

Actions must be taken once business owners are aware of them, as ignoring or postponing to take action may lead to deterioration of worker health and loss of productivity.

Working with AI systems may disrupt health in future like never imagined, and everyone concerned with worker health and wellness must be aware of these. Medico-legal cases may rise. The management must take appropriate steps once alerted by the OH physician of the possibility that workers working with AI systems may have health issues that can reduce productivity.

16

Fatigue amongst pilots: An Occupational Health and Safety concern

(published on 20th September, 2023 in www.occupationist.com)

Fatigue is a feeling of being extremely tired. It is a feeling of constant exhaustion, burnout or lack of energy. Fatigue is associated with a strong feeling of sleepiness.

Everyone is aware that fatigue can lead to accidents, wrong decisions etc. Yet people try to behave bold, and even drive personal vehicles as well as public transport vehicles including bus, trucks and aircrafts when fatigued due to lack of sleep. This attitude should change.

Pilots are no exceptions to fatigue – in fact, they are most affected and errors during flying cost lives, reputation and fear among air travelers.

Fatigue affects every adult at some point of their life. Most of the time fatigue is transient, yet it brings, for example, almost 1.5 million (15 lakhs) Australians to their doctor.

Pilots are no exceptions to fatigue – in fact, they are most affected and errors during flying cost lives, reputation and fear among air travelers.

The International Air Transport Association (IATA), a global grouping of airlines, including from India have long identified fatigue as a potential safety risk and the industry developed extensive Standards and Recommended Practices (SARPs) around managing fatigue risk. However, they are not followed strictly.

Additionally, under the fatigue reporting system, an Indian pilot can report to the Safety department of the airline concerned and the report is then sent to the Directorate General of Civil Aviation (DGCA).

For example, a senior captain from a leading airline based in India said the silent danger of fatigue needs to be addressed more aggressively as it affects one's cognitive abilities and psychological conditions.

IndiGo airlines became the first airline in India to use a gadget that can detect fatigue and alertness level before and after flights.

The captain further told PTI (Press Trust of India) that doing two consecutive nights of duty in multiple sectors most of the time results in fatigue and the existing fatigue reporting system is not popular among pilots.

In a recent survey of 542 pilots by NGO, Safety Matters Foundation, it was found that pilots admitted to falling asleep without planning or consent of the other crew member and had even experienced micro sleep. These observations make fatigue is a worrying issue for the fast-growing Indian aviation sector.

The pilots in India and in most other countries are tested for alcohol levels. However, they were not tested for fatigue levels. Recently, IndiGo airlines became the first airline in India to use a gadget that can detect fatigue and alertness level before and after flights. Meanwhile, the existing system where pilots can ask to be removed from flight duty if feeling tired will continue.

The fatigue test using the gadget takes about 5 minutes.

IndiGo will also have a sleep researcher to improve its fatigue management system. The gadget is from Thales, a French company.

It is hoped that other airlines in India as well as in other countries will follow the IndiGo example.

Ashim Mitra, senior VP (Flight Operations) at IndiGo in a communication to pilots said, 'After years of research, Thales have developed a fatigue detection model, offering detailed insights into demographic data, including routes, pairing, crew profiles and more, going beyond traditional scheduling models.'

Mitra further added, 'this initiative positions us at the forefront of airline safety and innovation, setting an industry standard. It also underscores our commitment to our pilots' wellbeing, ensuring their health, mental wellbeing, and job satisfaction, ultimately ensuring passenger safety.'

When leaders talk about wellness to their employees, sleep should be a starting point, rather than nutrition or exercise!

Fatigue management is in the domain of Occupational Health. Whether it is flying aircrafts, running inter-city transport buses or trucks, driving personal vehicles, working in shifts in factories or nuclear reactors, fatigue management should be an important consideration in managing employee health as well as in accident prevention.

In the energy companies that I worked (Shell, bp), fatigue management (FM) courses were offered to all employees involved in driving (even personal cars) and in any other dangerous operations. Such initiatives not only demonstrate an image of a responsible employer but also transmit a message about safety at work. Fatigue also reduces productivity and having FM in place mitigates it.

Fatigue is an indication of an underlying illness (including occupational illness) which can lead to industrial or vehicular (including aircrafts) accidents. When industrial accidents happen, the press and the people do not over-react once they know that the organization had systems (like Fatigue Management) in place, thus mitigating any reputational harm due to an accident.

A fatigue detection gadget should be made an important requirement in hazardous industries as much as an AED as more lives will be saved due to industrial as well as vehicular accidents.

Years ago, Dr David Flower, an Occupational Health physician, had done extensive work in alertness management in long-haul flying for flight and cabin crew. In 2000, he was a member of the British Olympic Association's Acclimatization Working Party, advising the British Olympic team on the management of jetlag in preparation for the Sydney Olympics in 2000. This was to improve performance among sportspersons.

An Occupational Health (OH) physician can be an immensely resourceful contributor in managing fatigue management in a company's operation along with safety professionals.

It is important to know that fatigue is a symptom and not a medical condition. Fatigue can be mental or physical or a combination of both. It can be transient, cumulative or circadian. It can be physiologic, secondary or chronic. Hence it is important to find out the reasons in an individual complaining of fatigue, so that it can be prevented.

An Occupational Health physician can be an immensely resourceful contributor in managing fatigue management in a company's operation.

There are many medical conditions (anemia, depression, fibromyalgia, chronic diseases of kidney, liver or lung, viral or bacterial infection) that can cause fatigue but it is equally important to check if it is due to lack of sleep. This is because transient fatigue is more common and is due to extreme lack of sleep or extended awake hours within 24 to 48 hours; and is a major cause of serious accidents.

A fatigue detection gadget should be made an important requirement in hazardous industries as much as an AED as more lives will be saved due to industrial as well as vehicular accidents. Occupational Health physicians should impress upon the management to invest in such a device.

Wellbeing at workplace: Survey of Indian employee

(published on 14th September, 2023 in www.occupationist.com)

A recent joint report by two job providing website companies – Indeed and Forrester Consulting has found that more than 3 out of 4 of all workers in India reported low levels of wellbeing.

The global average of thriving employees (that is, employees who experience high levels of wellbeing) is around 25 percent. In India the above report translates it to 24 percent, making Indian organizations almost at par with global average of thriving employees.

Work culture varies from companies to companies and countries to countries, and within the same company operating in different geographies.

What does it mean by high levels of wellbeing or thriving employees. University of Oxford Wellness Research Centre has outlined certain traits to categorise employees with high levels of wellbeing who 'thrive at work,' namely,

- notable job satisfaction,
- minimal work-related stress,
- heightened positivity/happiness,
- a distinct sense of purpose within their organisational role

The other aspects highlighted by the survey report were:

- 67 percent or more employees mentioned that their employers are responsible for their wellbeing at work. These workplaces are marked by inclusivity, acceptance, respectful interactions, and supportive management.
- Among the professionals surveyed, 93 percent reported their managers exhibiting empathetic leadership,
- 87 percent of these professionals indicated that their managers lead by example.
- 69 percent of surveyed employees noted that senior leadership in their organisations expects them to take on additional responsibilities.

Now, these findings in the survey are not seen often, as there are many studies on workplace culture in India that indicate otherwise.

People (including employees) measure their wellbeing status with their friends and colleagues. That is why wellness programs should include peers (at workplace) to compare themselves to.

Those who lead wellness programs should aim to raise the bar and devise strategies to incrementally improve the percentage of thriving employees in their organizations.

"Wellbeing at work is an integral part of our daily lives, whether we're working remotely or in the office. Our findings indicate that emphasis on wellbeing at work will only increase going forward," Sashi Kumar, Head of Sales, Indeed India, said.

Everyone right from the top management to executioners and beneficiaries should interact to incrementally improve the percentage of thriving employees from the current levels.

Work culture varies from companies to companies and countries to countries, and within the same company operating in different geographies. This is because work culture is a reflection of the various norms and standards followed by its people. That is why customization of wellness programs is important.

Managers leading the wellness programs must consider local norms and a discussion with employees regarding what they want and share associated health benefits, both short-term and long-term. These are some of the recipes for success of a wellness program.

The author believes that since wellness is all about health, non-medical managers leading a wellness program may make a big success out of it if inputs are sought from a doctor, or more specifically an Occupational Health physician.

Running a wellness program is teamwork - and everyone right from the top management to executioners and beneficiaries should interact to incrementally improve the percentage of thriving employees from the current levels. Wellness programs have other agendas as well (stop smoking, weight reduction etc.) and all these must show an upward improvement trend. That is truly the success of a wellness program.

Organizations must keep this in mind at the outset and regular interactions must take place between the person leading the wellness program, an Occupational Health physician (if he/she is not the one leading it) and most importantly with the employees. Employee feedback should be respected, and changes made as the program progresses. Wellness programs should be dynamic.

Finally, it is also important for decision makers to remember that people (including employees) measure their wellbeing status with their friends and colleagues. That is why wellness programs should include peers (at workplace) to compare themselves to. Every participant in a wellness program should be rewarded – those who are consistent, be rewarded a little more.

18

The future of work in extreme heat

(published on 7th September, 2023 in www.occupationist.com)

In the US and the Western European nations, July 2023 was a month of extreme heat rarely experienced by their citizens. This led to around 150 deaths in just 5 counties of American states. While writing this article, Maricopa County in Phoenix, for example, has 312 deaths still under investigation for a possible heat-related cause.

More heat leads to more deaths especially in a population that isn't used to it. In the tropical countries the heat is much more but the deaths are proportionately fewer as they are better acclimatised. And even those few deaths in tropical countries are mainly due to lack of timely awareness, lack of shade areas, lack of cool, potable drinking water and lack of timely government advisory.

Industry leaders usually follow government advisories, if at all.

More heat leads to more deaths especially in a population that isn't used to it.

Scientists have cautioned that heat waves will continue to get worse with the climate crisis. It is the greenhouse gas emissions that will lead to extreme heat in future.

Extreme heat not only causes discomfort but also leads to productivity losses. In vulnerable population, extreme heat causes death.

David S. Jones, a physician and historian at Harvard University, said the numbers reported here and more widely across the country are likely underestimates. He called the counts "mysterious." "The low numbers of reported death really puzzle me," Jones told CNN. "Less severe heat waves in the US have killed hundreds of people in the past. I think it is very likely that the current mortality reports from the US in summer of 2023 are a significant undercount, though I have no proof of that."

In India, by around 2100, it is estimated that 1.5 million more people will likely die every year as a result of climate change; this is as high as deaths from all infectious diseases in India today. This was revealed in an October 2019 study by the Climate Impact Lab.

The study further said, with continued high greenhouse gas emissions, the average annual temperature in India is estimated to increase from 24 to 28 degrees C by end of this century.

The other finding of the study was that the number of extremely hot days per year are expected to increase. By 2100 there would be 42 days with temperature over 35 degrees C increasing from about 5 per year in 2010.

Kamal Kishore, member of National Management Disaster Authority, had said at the release of the report on October 31 2019, "These findings are a reminder that we have to keep making concerted, long-term efforts to build resilience to extreme heat."

The future of outdoor work in extreme hot climate is a matter of concern. Governments and industry leaders should make every effort to curb greenhouse gas emissions. On the other hand, scientists, researchers and Occupational Health physicians should constantly remind the law makers, industry leaders and the public to be aware of this stark reality and take appropriate timely actions.

The International Labour Organisation (ILO) in its July 2019 report said that productivity loss due to heat stress in India, brought on by rapidly rising temperatures, will be equivalent to 34 million full-time jobs in another 10 years.

The ILO also reiterated that agriculture and construction work are expected to suffer the most. And that is bad news for India where farming and construction are the top two occupations, both of which are unorganized and are done outdoors where workers also work for long hours.

In India, there are millions of outdoor workers who are already finding it difficult to work as temperatures rise every year, harming their health and hurting productivity.

The future of outdoor work in extreme hot climate is a matter of concern. Governments and industry leaders should make every effort to curb greenhouse gas emissions. On the other hand, scientists, researchers and Occupational Health physicians should constantly remind the law makers, industry leaders and the public to be aware of this stark reality and take appropriate timely actions.

Greenhouse emissions are directly related to population growth as uncontrolled population leads to increase in consumption.

To mitigate the issue of productivity loss and health effects of extreme heat (death, discomfort, safety issues), a multi-pronged approach is needed that includes population control, mechanization of agriculture and construction, awareness in all sections of society and timely advisories by the government about the steps to be taken to manage health effects due to heat.

The OH physician should create awareness in the industry he/she works and issue timely advisories (relating to extreme heat and other relevant health issues) to the employees.

19

Eye discomfort at workplace: Take steps now

(published on 21st August, 2023 in www.occupationist.com)

Eye discomfort use to happen even a few decades ago but were much lesser and the reasons were different. Eye discomforts were found in the elderly, those doing a lot of data entering work in register books, and due to inadequate (dim) lighting.

Good lighting is important in reducing eye discomfort.

In the last few years, lighting has improved but not the glare. In fact, the glare has increased and so the glare time. Mobile phones, computers and TV are the biggest sources of glare. The register books are gone – today all data is fed in the computer.

The various eye discomforts a worker can have are enumerated below:

- eyestrain (eye pain)
- dry eyes
- blurred vision
- red or pink eyes
- burning in the eyes
- light sensitivity
- headaches

Over the years, lighting has improved but not the glare. In fact, the glare has increased and so the glare time.

Eye discomfort is caused by:

- poor lighting
- glare on a computer or mobile phone screen
- dim lighting and too much brightness on the computer or mobile phone screen
- poor quality computer or mobile phone screen (e.g., poor resolution, blurry image, etc.)
- poor seating posture
- incorrect viewing distance
- uncorrected prior vision
- dry air
- ventilation
- indoor air quality
- a combination of the above factors

Indoor air quality impacts the comfort of the eye due to following:

- Indoor air contaminants - chemicals, dusts, moulds or fungi, bacteria, gases, vapours, odours etc.
- Indoor environment - temperature, humidity, air circulation, ventilation
- Inadequate air intake from outside

Just as industries having high-noise areas have hearing conservation program, it is worth considering having an 'eye protection program' in factories and offices.

Good lighting is important in reducing eye discomfort. Lighting audit will assure if lighting in the workplace is adequate or not. Lights shouldn't be dim or too bright that it is difficult to read printed documents.

Most offices have computers that lead to not only just eye problems but musculoskeletal problems (like neck pain, back pain, carpal tunnel syndrome etc.) as well that can be mitigated by observing the following steps:

- Take adequate breaks (I suggest stretching in the chair after 30-40 minutes followed by getting up from the chair, walking around for a minute and viewing a distant object before getting back to the seat)
- Avoid viewing the computer screen from a close distance and for a longer time
- Avoid any glare hitting the computer screen; rectify it
- Ensure adequate ambient lighting
- Make Workstation (computer, chair, keyboard, mouse etc.) comfortable
- Check vision to avoid eyestrain (see an optician once every year or two)
- Room or hall to have colour variety

Just as industries having high-noise areas have hearing conservation program to protect hearing of workers who are working in high-noise areas, it is worth considering having an 'eye protection program' not only in factories (to protect workers from getting hurt due to flying objects) but also in offices.

Take few of the self-steps proactively and you may not have to see a doctor reactively!

The Occupational Health physician, whose primary responsibility is to proactively prevent illnesses happening due to work, workplace or working conditions, would recommend the following simple steps to mitigate eye discomfort as part of 'eye protection program.'

- Adequate breaks: Create awareness in employees about the significance of taking frequent breaks. There are software available that prompt you to take breaks – follow them. In absence of any such software embedded in your computer, I suggest getting up from the chair after about 30-40 minutes of work, blinking the eyes, stretching for a while, walking a few steps in the room, viewing a distant object like a tree, and then returning back to the chair. Even while working with computers, it is advisable to look away from the screen for a few seconds.

- Lighting in the room/hall: Lighting should be such that it does not strain the eyes during normal work.
- Glare: Make sure there is no glare either from the windows or shiny floors and walls. Use blinds (curtains) in the windows and matte finish tiles on the floor and paints on the wall.
- Monitor: The brightness and contrast of the monitor should not hurt the eyes. If viewing the monitor hurts or strains the eyes, adjust the brightness and contrast. Make sure there is no glare hitting the monitor screen.

In the absence of an OH physician, the proactive steps as mentioned above, if taken, are useful not just due to mitigate eye discomfort due to work, workplace or working conditions but even otherwise – as the screen time and hence the glare has increased due to advent of smart phones and other gaming devices.

If you have eye discomfort that persists after taking the above-mentioned self-steps, see an optician (or an eye specialist).

Take few of the self-steps proactively (prominent among them being making sure the room your work is ventilated, is clean and free of dust and moulds, and has adequate lighting), and you may not have to see a doctor reactively!

20

Can office design influence your health and wellbeing?

(published on 9th August, 2023 in www.occupationist.com)

The 21st century has seen offices undergo changes in their look and feel. It started with cubicles giving way to open offices. By 2015, offices had ping pong and foosball tables. Even small offices with the constraints of space and budget offered some wellness activity to their employees, like a small fish tank. The idea was to keep employee health and wellbeing in good stead.

Occasionally it is some trigger at workplace that sets the tone for a wellness program or to establish Occupational Health practices in an organization. The trigger could be, say, death of an employee due to lack of dealing with a medical emergency at workplace. Absence of provisions to manage such a contingency; no first-aiders, no AED, no ambulance tie-up etc. increases noise in the organization creating reputational issues which then forces the management to think about employee wellness at workplace. Whenever a non-accidental death (NAD) investigation is done, and it should be done with more regularity, it may indicate that the deceased had medical problems found in a previous medical check that were unattended. Any risk identified during a NAD investigation should be promptly addressed and followed-up for its robustness.

By 2015, offices had ping pong and foosball tables.

Little is known about why, where and when did employers begin to consider office design as a tool to employee health and wellbeing. While sweatshops were thriving in Europe and Americas in the name of industrial revolution there was one industrialist in India, Jamsetji Tata who thought about employee welfare as early as 1877 when he opened the Empress Mills at Nagpur.

Few in the world are aware that the with the opening of Empress Mills about 140 years ago, the greatest contribution of Jamsetji Tata was the visionary standards it set for worker welfare.

The author believes that whoever leads the changes in office redesign, beneath it unknown to them was functioning a medical specialty that few know and understand – Occupational Health, yet everyone practices in some form or the other. Every responsible leader has tried to improve the health of its employees working in various occupations in the organization, based on experience, beliefs, vision, compassion, and advice – it is a mix but the willingness to take actions is paramount.

Employees enjoy a well-designed workplace as it is less stressful to them.

Occupational Health, in short, is a medical specialty that deals with everything to protect worker health due to the work, workplace and working conditions.

Sometimes employers have an agenda for worker welfare and are often guided by keen sense of awareness and compassion towards people working for their enterprise and the willingness to take action to ease the pain of the worker. I have read about Jamsetji Tata and Ratan Tata demonstrating these three qualities – awareness, compassion, and willingness.

Employees enjoy a well-designed workplace as it is less stressful to them. The employees relate positively with the management who considers providing a well-designed workplace with the requisite facilities. This leads to an environment conducive to employees giving their best to the organization. Hence, employers should be sensitive to employee expectations and the benefits gained thereof.

Yet there are a lot of organizations that do not provide healthy workplaces. The following are the findings of the Fellowes Workplace Wellness Trend report:

- 87% of workers would like their current employer to offer healthier workspace benefits, with options ranging from wellness rooms, company fitness benefits, sit-stands, healthy lunch options and ergonomic seating.
- Employees of younger companies are less likely (34%) to be turned down when asking for in-office benefits like sit-stand desks, than employees at established companies (42%).
- 93% of workers in the tech industry said they would stay longer at a company who would offer healthier workspace benefits, with options ranging from wellness rooms, company fitness benefits, sit-stands, healthy lunch options and ergonomic seating.

A big drawback of open offices is that the need for privacy during some calls, personal or official which often causes interference and a frustrating experience. Some offices have kiosks where employees can make calls requiring privacy.

Workplace design should have DIE (Diversity, Inclusiveness & Equity) considerations that accounts for female gender, breast feeding rooms, creche etc. Consideration should also be given to trans gender employees and those with physical challenges.

Keeping employee concerns in mind, an international organization has established requirements to create productive and comfortable indoor environments. The WELL Building Standard™ (WELL) is the premier standard for buildings, interior spaces and communities seeking to implement, validate and measure features that support and advance human health and wellness.

Administered by the International WELL Building Institute (IWBITM), and certified by Green Business Certification Inc., the WELL Building Standard is the first that focuses on human health and wellbeing into design, construction and operations of buildings. According to the IWBITM, workplace design that considers air quality, lighting, views onto nature and the general layout of the interior can significantly impact on health, satisfaction, wellbeing and staff productivity.

The WELL Building Standard focuses on seven concepts of building performance: Air, Water, Nourishment, Light, Fitness, Comfort and Mind. Implementation of WELL requires multi-functional approach and the role of Occupational Health (OH) physician is important as the entire exercise is to improve worker health and wellness, and hence productivity. Corporations not employing OH physicians should reach out to external sources for advice.

In addition, workplace design should have DIE (Diversity, Inclusiveness & Equity) considerations that accounts for female gender, breast feeding rooms, creche etc. Consideration should also be given to trans gender employees and those with physical challenges. Research has shown that workplace design can positively influences health, wellbeing, employee satisfaction, and performance. Every workplace has a potential for improving and making a positive impact on employee wellbeing. By offering employees areas to recharge and taking their comfort into consideration, the offices can have an improved environment.

Preventing 'take-home toxins' from being taken from workplace

(published on 31st July, 2023 in www.occupationist.com)

Hazards at workplace should remain at workplace; they shouldn't come home. Responsible workplaces have a method to contain these hazards while mitigating them. When workplace hazards come home, they rub on the family members and cause them harm – and that's not a nice thing.

A worker can bring home, unknowingly, many hazardous substances depending on their workplace and working conditions, on their clothes, skin, footwear, accessories (mobile phone, wallet etc.) and even in vehicle interiors.

Family members are vulnerable to these workplace toxins, which can hide in furniture, laundry, circulate in the entire house and spread by person-to-person contact.

Workplace toxins have health impacts that could be temporary or permanent. Symptoms of toxicity may arise years after initial exposure. The exposure to workplace toxins could be insidious or gradual but health effects may be seen after a long time.

For example, lead is one toxin that can cause physical and mental developmental issues in children due to chronic exposure. In high doses, lead is fatal. According to EPA (Environmental Protection Agency, USA), 'lead from paint, including lead-contaminated dust, is one of the most common causes of lead poisoning.'

Family members are vulnerable to these workplace toxins, which can hide in furniture, laundry, circulate in the entire house and spread by person-to-person contact.

Industries like construction, manufacturing, mining, transportation, agriculture, pesticide are most likely to make the workers to take home workplace toxins unless strict steps are taken to prevent.

Take home toxins (THT) can be classified as:

- Chemical (Asbestos, Arsenic, Lead, Silica, Fiberglass, Pesticide etc.)
- Biological (animal waste, infectious agents etc.)
- Radioactive
- Psychological (work stress, bullying, promotions etc.)

Psychological classification is not a 'thing' that can be classified as a toxin but in reality, it is. I view psychological hazard at workplace as a 'take home toxin' because a psychological hazard (stress) affecting a worker at workplace usually rubs into family members and causes subtle psychological issues at home that have a tendency to become chronic and serious.

OSHA (Occupational Health and Safety Administration) USA has standards that are aimed at preventing take-home toxins in construction (1926.62) and general industry (1910.1025). OSHA can impose fines on employers who don't follow them.

Requirements in these standards include:

- Providing workers a place to change into clean clothes after work to avoid contaminating their personal clothes
- Providing appropriate shower and hand washing facilities
- Controlling dust and fumes in workplace
- Testing the worksite for hazards

- Administering proper training to workers

I may add at least one more: have a zero-tolerance policy for those who indulge in spreading toxic culture at workplace.

Employers should make sure that workers are provided with the right PPE to avoid workplace toxins coming into contact with the garments beneath. Employers should also ensure employees don't leave the workplace wearing the clothes they wore while working.

No workplace toxin (hazard) should come home, and employers must ensure workers get regular, trustworthy, dependable and well-supervised protection.

Business owners should seek advice from Occupational Health physicians and Industrial Hygienists to check if there are workplace toxins in the industries they operate and take appropriate steps as outlined above to prevent 'take-home toxins' being taken from workplace to homes.

Family members should also be aware of the idea of 'take-home toxins' and politely but regularly ask the worker before entering home if s/he had de-toxified while leaving the workplace. This habit of family members will ensure that the worker in a hurry to come back home de-toxifies at workplace thus preventing illnesses amongst family members.

Awareness and taking appropriate steps to mitigate the effects of take-home toxins will reduce the incidence of a lot of illnesses in the worker, the families, and communities.

No workplace toxin (hazard) should come home, and employers must ensure workers get regular, trustworthy, dependable and well-supervised protection.

Occupational Health issues in call-centre workers

(published on 25th July, 2023 in www.occupationist.com)

Every occupation has the potential to cause injuries and illnesses in workers. It is immaterial if the worker is from the top management or otherwise; is white-collared or otherwise.

In a high-profile industry, depending on the job, the robot is both the new blue-collar as well as the white-collar worker!

With introduction of technology, many erstwhile blue-collar workers in high-profile industries are now white-collared, except in fishing, construction, and agriculture where we still find blue collar workers, especially in developing countries, including India.

In a high-profile industry, depending on the job, the robot is both the new blue-collar as well as the white-collar worker!

Most call-centres employ thousands of workers – the initial impression is that these workers are well taken care of; as they are picked up and dropped at their homes, are given free meals and a reasonable compensation. The workplace also looks good and clean. But behind this glamour are a lot of unseen hazards that are capable of doing a lot of harm to physical and mental health of a worker in a call-centre worker.

Like any other occupation, the call-centre workers have their share of work-related illnesses. The sad part is that due to paucity of doctors specialized in diseases of occupations, their work-related health issues usually go unaddressed. The call-centres seldom employ or consult Occupational Health (OH) physicians who are experts in diseases of occupations.

Banking and finance, insurance, travel services, telecommunications, road services, utilities, and sales are some of the common industries that depend on their businesses on call centres. The main function of a call centre is to provide customer service through telephone or computer.

The usual tasks done by a person in a call centre include the following:

- Provide information and product support and information to clients/customers by landline phone using a headset
- Answer or dial telephone and/or electronic requests and resolve customer complaints
- Manage aggressive behavior or other issues of a dissatisfied customer

The health hazards for a call centre employee are:

Biological:

- Infections may spread if workstations (desks) of coworkers are close to each other.
- Infections also spread when desks and equipment are shared without cleaning between uses.

Physical:

- Air quality in the room or hall could be poor leading to fatigue.
- Noise exposure due to fellow worker talking or an acoustic incident through the headset (e.g., crackles, whistles, hisses or high-pitched sounds, feedback, or phone receivers being accidently dropped).

- Inadequate regulation of room temperature can lead to heat and cold stress.

Chemical:

- Like any other office-based employee, call centre employees may be exposed to chemicals emanating from cleaning products, photocopier toner, and other products.

Ergonomic:

- Musculo-skeletal disorders due to sitting for long hours.
- Continuous typing or doing the same work leads to RSIs (Repetitive Strain Injury).
- Inadequate lighting (e.g., glare, low level lighting, etc.) may cause workers adopting awkward postures leading to aches and pains. Glare can also lead to headache or trigger a pre-existing migraine.
- Small workplaces also cause workers to adopt awkward postures leading to aches and pains. It can also lead to claustrophobic feeling.

Psychosocial:

- Threats of violence, harassment, verbal or sexual abuse by the online customer.
- Lone working: sometimes there are few workers in the call centre, and all busy. This can lead to a sense of loneliness.
- Workplace stress due to performance targets, monetary incentives for increased output, quotas, targets, or demands from the customers.
- Shift work can lead to certain health issues in the long run. The workers should follow advices on how they can be reduced.

Others:

- Voice fatigue due to extensive talking (total or intermittent loss of voice, changes in pitch and decrease in voice volume, constant throat clearing, drying in the throat and excessive mucous, the sensation of a lump or pain in the throat, increased effort to talk).
- Difficulty in swallowing due to prolonged talking.
- Shortness of breath may be a result of talking without resting the voice.
- Overeating (as food is usually provided free) and excessive hours of continuous sitting (part of their job) places them at a higher risk of lifestyle diseases, namely, diabetes, hypertension, weight gain etc.

The hazards in call-centres are more or less the same. Having identified the hazards, its mitigation is of paramount importance to lower the harm to a call-centre employee health to as low as reasonably practicable (ALARP). This is an area where expertise of an Occupational Health physician helps along with HR and Admin.

Discussing each and every hazard and its mitigation is out of the scope of this article.

———————

23

Diversity and Inclusion in Occupational Health

(published on 30th June, 2023 in www.occupationist.com)

Until few years back, Occupational Health (OH) essentially was one glove fits all – there were hardly any variations from the standard. But we now live in the world engulfed by the term D&I and with the advent of Gen Z at workplace in large numbers, the HR and Health professionals employed by the company are modifying their health, wellness and benefits policies which are nothing but subsets of OH.

A workplace that cares well often fares well.

With more newer employees in offices than in factories today, the demography of workers is distinct though overlapping.

There are four generations of workers in an office today – the baby boomers, the Gen X, the Millennials and the Gen Z. These terms are social generations of the western world, now, being used globally.

For the unversed, baby boomers are those born between 1946 and 1964. Gen X are those born between 1965 and 1981, Millennials are those born between 1981 and 1996, lastly, Gen Z are those born between 1997 and 2012. Those born after 2012 are Gen Alpha and are yet to enter the job market.

The Gen Alpha might pose challenges at workforce which we can't even imagine now.

The Gen Alpha will start entering the workforce around 2033 onwards. The Gen Alpha might pose challenges at workforce which we can't even imagine now.

Without defining, it becomes easy to understand D & I if one reads Verna Myers famous quote, 'Diversity is being invited to the party. Inclusion is being asked to dance.' Verna Myers is a well-known diversity advocate.

When we talk about diversity in OH it means that health concerns of everyone (based on age, gender, physical ability, thought process etc.) in the workforce have been accounted for.

Inclusion in OH would mean that the health policies have taken into consideration benefits and health status of all employees and have been shared with them to be able to be productive and contribute safely to the organization, without harming one's health or of the coworkers.

Gen Z, also called Zoomers, comprise around 25% of workforce and the percentage is increasing. Their expectations from workplace are different. Most are tech savvy with different levels of expertise. The recent Covid pandemic also forced the less savvy Zoomers to embrace the digital technology. As a result, they enjoy the idea of WoFA (work from anywhere).

A lot of Zoomers are financially independent and have a lot of disposable income. This makes them prone to develop habits that may be injurious to health, both in the short and long term; and hence awareness sessions and counseling should be available to prevent harm to health.

Habits such as smoking (poor respiratory health, cancer etc.), taking excessive alcohol (liver failure, drink & drive issues etc.), eating unhealthy foods (metabolic disorders, obesity etc.), use of mobile phones (tech neck, eye strain etc.), working long hours with computers (eye strain, musculoskeletal disorders etc.), listening to loud music with earphones (hearing issues etc.) are some of the activities in Zoomers especially, as well as in others, that have the potential to cause many health issues enlisted in brackets. In addition, lack of sleep (fatigue, low concentration etc.), lack of exercise (metabolic disorders etc.), increased consumerism (mental health etc.) all impact health.

Workplace is an apt place where the Zoomers and the Millennials could be guided to responsible living and not get into any premature health issues, sometimes irreversible or difficult/expensive to treat. Many of the diseases, both work-related and others can be easily prevented if there is awareness and timely intervention. If this is not done, both local and global burden of disease increases.

For business leaders, when it comes to matters of health of their employees, what is required is awareness (observation), compassion and willingness to take action.

Guiding the Zoomers and even the Millennials in matters of health may be viewed as a wellness initiative by the senior management. In-house physician(s) in an office can devise programs to tackle the specific problems of the Zoomers and Millennials. The health checks for the Zoomers and Millennials need not be annual but should include tests and consultations based on individual risk profile.

One glove fits all approach for health checks specifically for Zoomers and Millennials and generally for all employees in the workplace do not yield expected outcomes. The health checks have to be customised for each employee depending on age, gender, work, past history, family history etc.

The guidance regarding prevention is usually provided by in-house doctors (OH physicians who are trained in preventing diseases proactively) in large offices and factories.

In smaller offices and factories, including MSMEs (Micro, Small, Medium Enterprises), services of external medical specialists should be sought. In fact, some of these smaller enterprises do hire part-time doctors to manage their work-related health concerns.

I am reminded of Jamsetji Tata who in 1877 (around 145 years ago) thought of creche, ventilation, gym, medical facilities etc. in his first cotton mill, the Empress Mills at Nagpur. He also ensured separate dispensaries for men and women, surely an example of D & I for that era. The mill also held a Health Week each year to highlight various diseases and how workers could keep themselves and their families safe.

For business leaders, when it comes to matters of health of their employees, what is required is awareness (observation), compassion and willingness to take action. This is echoed by what Jamsetji Tata said in 1895, 'we do not claim to be more unselfish, more generous or more philanthropic than other people. But, we think, we started on sound and straightforward business principles, considering the interest of our shareholders our own, and the health and welfare of our employees the sure foundation of our prosperity.'

A workplace that cares well often fares well.

Air-conditioned truck drivers' cabin in India:
An Occupational Health Initiative

(published on 24th June, 2023 in www.occupationist.com)

On 20th June 2023, the Indian Road Transport and Highways Minister Nitin Gadkari signed the file that mandates air-conditioning in truck driver cabins.

Addressing the event called 'Desh Chaalak - Recognising those who move India,' the Minister said, 'Our drivers operate vehicles in harsh temperatures of 43 to 47 degrees Centigrade and we must imagine the condition of drivers. I was keen to introduce the AC cabin after I became a minister. But some people opposed it saying the cost of trucks will go up. Today, I have signed the file that all truck cabins will be AC cabins.'

The event 'Desh Chaalak - Recognising those who move India' was organised by Mahindra Logistics.

Nitin Gadkari also spoke about shortage of drivers in India, resulting in truckers operating 14-16 hours a day. He said, 'In other countries, there is a restriction on the number of hours a trucker can be on duty,' he said.

In his address, Union Minister Nitin Gadkari reiterated about the reduction in logistic costs in India and the need to be brought down in order to improve export competitiveness – adding good quality roads and trucks is the key to it.

Business leaders and governments should understand that many of the actions they take are Occupational Health (OH) initiatives and taking inputs from OH specialists will help identify more areas requiring health, safety and productivity improvements.

It will interest the readers to know that the approach that the Union Minister Nitin Gadkari followed is what an Occupational Health (OH) physician does in the factory or office where he/she works. The OH physician finds out what are the hazards due to the work an employee does, if the workplace has any factors affecting health and if there are any specific working conditions that can impact health.

Occupational Health is a medical specialty that proactively controls recognized hazards and identifies unrecognized hazards present due to the nature of work, at workplace or due to working conditions that can affect health and find ways to reduce them to ALARP (as low as reasonably practicable).

Similar approach was undertaken by the Indian Prime Minister Narendra Modi when he made provision for cooking gas to replace wood, especially in rural India or when MS Dhoni, the Indian cricketer took a nap on the floor of an airport to make up for a sleep deficit. These are examples of looking for hazards that can affect health, work and performance, and then taking steps to reduce the impact of hazards on health and to improve performance.

For a business or a political leader, sometimes it is just about being alert to a hazardous situation, being compassionate to the sufferings of the people working and be willing to take action to reduce the impact of hazards to safeguard health, improve productivity and create a safety culture.

The approach undertaken by the Indian Prime Minister Narendra Modi to replace burning of wood and provide cooking gas, especially in rural India and MS Dhoni, the Indian cricketer taking a nap on the floor of an airport to make up for a sleep deficit are nothing but OH initiatives to improve health and performance.

The workplace of the driver is the truck and more specifically the cabin where he/she sits, sometimes for hours, to do the work of driving. Not only should the cabin be air-conditioned but the seat must be ergonomically designed for better sitting comfort. In addition, any control panel should be within easy reach so that adjustments can be easily made. Working conditions for a driver which needs to be addressed include work hours, rest breaks, road quality, buddy driver in case of long driving etc. If all these are taken care of, the drivers' health is kept in good stead, productivity improves and so does road safety records.

For a business or a political leader, sometimes it is just about being alert to a hazardous situation, being compassionate to the sufferings of the people working and be willing to take action to reduce the impact of hazards to safeguard health, improve productivity and create a safety culture.

Business leaders and governments should understand that many of the actions they take are OH initiatives and taking inputs from OH specialists will help identify more areas where actions to alleviate work-related health issues are to be taken, in addition to productivity gains and safe working. After all, an estimated 20% of all patients seen by a GP are illnesses caused by work and the access to OH in most workplaces, including the unorganised sector, is low to nil in almost every country. Truck drivers, sadly, are a part of unorganised sector.

AI, U & OI

(published on 19th June, 2023 in www.occupationist.com)

It is basically about how AI (Artificial Intelligence) affects U (you) and can potentially cause OI (Occupational Illnesses).

Yes, AI can cause OI. How? Let us understand...

AI is around 60 years old. At the beginning of 1950, John Von Neumann and Alan Turing were the founding fathers of the technology behind AI. The term AI could be attributed to John McCarthy of MIT (Massachusetts Institute of Technology, USA).

Herbert Simon, economist and sociologist, prophesied in 1957 that the AI would succeed in beating a human at chess in the next 10 years. Simon's vision proved to be right as the success in May 1997 of Deep Blue (IBM's expert system) at the chess game against Garry Kasparov fulfilled Herbert Simon's 1957 prophecy 40 years later.

However, there was no one to support the financing and development of this form of AI.

AI improves safety but can create unsafe work parameters of working leading to work-related (occupational) illnesses and accidents.

The operation of Deep Blue was based on a systematic brute force algorithm in which all possible moves were accounted for. The human defeat was symbolic in history but Deep Blue had only managed a very limited scope regarding the rules of the chess game compared to the complexities of the world.

The new boom in AI started around 2010 due to massive volumes of data and very high efficiency of computer graphics card processors.

From no support in 1997, overnight, around 2010, research teams all over the world turned to this technology with benefits mankind had never imagined or thought about.

With regards to AI at workplace, the Covid pandemic accelerated the deployment of AI-based tools. One of the areas was employee monitoring.

The Covid pandemic forced many to work remotely. To monitor their wellbeing and work output many employers used technological tools that includes monitoring of internet access, using webcams, keystroke logging, time-tracking devices etc.

It was ok during the pandemic as it was a question of survival for everyone. Now that the pandemic is over, there are concerns that such monitoring is intrusive, excessive and overwhelming.

And in situations where AI is used to assess workloads, it may push workers harder than what a line manager would do to perform more tasks, faster. This happens because the background data says such workloads are theoretically possible. This can impact worker health especially if workers' physical and mental strength have not been assessed.

AI improves safety but can create unsafe work parameters of working, due to lack of 'prevention through design' approach including automatic algorithm system, leading to work-related (occupational) illnesses and accidents.

In August 2022, the European Agency for Safety and Health at Work (OSHA) had released a report that examined the risks and opportunities presented by AI-based worker management systems and their impact.

The report found that AI can enable better monitoring of hazards and mental health of workers.

AI also contributes in improving safety at workplace – by human error reduction, automation of dangerous tasks, harassment monitoring, equipment integrity, crime detection and prevention, in offices and factories.

The report also listed the dangers that it can pose; briefly summarized as follows:

- AI usage can 'dehumanise' workers by giving the sense that they have very limited control over their jobs.
- Usage of AI at workplace can also create unhealthy and pressured environment with little transparency about how decisions can be made or challenged.
- AI usage can create mistrust, limit worker participation and lead to work-life balance issues.
- AI also can cause serious mental and physical harm, including anxiety, musculoskeletal and cardiovascular disorders.

The report suggested that employers should pursue 'prevention through design' approach from the start. The design includes, among other things automatic algorithm system that is used for assignment of work and rating of worker performance.

In summer of 2021 food delivery company Deliveroo was fined by the Grante, the Italian data protection authority. It said that Deliveroo collected a disproportionate amount of personal data from its riders, in violation of the EU General Data Protection Regulation. This data was used for the automated rating of each rider's performance and for the assignment of work. The Garante found that Deliveroo was not transparent enough about how such algorithms worked.

Foodinho, another Italian food delivery company was fined because the workings of its automatic algorithm system, used to evaluate the performance of workers, were not sufficiently transparent and did not ensure accurate results.

To prevent mismatch of work requires that the AI is trained using adequate data and that humans (including workers, their line managers and even Occupational Health physicians) are involved in decision-making.

In the UK, in response to concerns over staff safety and data protection, the Information Commissioner's Office (ICO) issued draft guidance in October 2022 to help ensure employers' monitoring of staff performance doesn't turn into surveillance or harassment.

The ICO reminds companies they must make workers aware of the nature, extent and reasons for monitoring, and ensure it's proportionate. It says, 'Just because a form of monitoring is available, it does not mean it is the best way to achieve your aims.'

Anurag Bana, a senior project lawyer in the IBA's Legal Policy & Research Unit, says 'there needs to be an appropriate level of human oversight for any AI worker management system to protect employees' and that 'there should also be an algorithmic impact assessment procedure before any system is installed.' He believes that a human rights due diligence exercise in respect of AI systems is essential in order that 'automated decision-making does not produce harmful outcomes and workers can challenge how decisions are made to ensure transparency and accountability.'

The risk of AI is not ethics and compliance, but legal as well as reputational.

Bana says that employers need to demonstrate a duty of care to employees regarding AI use. 'Providing information to employees about how and why AI is being used is not enough,' he explains. 'There needs to be consultation with staff about the business reasons for using AI and how it will positively impact them. You need to have employees' buy-in before you start monitoring their performance in this way. You also should have an ethical framework in place that protects employees' health and safety – it may be a good idea to conduct an assessment/check compliance against the ISO 45003 guidelines, which look at employees' psychological health and safety at work.'

Johan Hübner, Chair of the IBA Artificial Intelligence and Robotics Subcommittee and a partner at Swedish law firm Delphi, says that 'excessive monitoring can lead to higher levels of employee stress and increased ill health among employees.'

Where AI is used to allocate tasks, it's 'important to ensure that all dimensions of the allocated tasks are included in the AI-generated decision,' adds Hübner.

In some countries, organisations could face fines and damages claims for injury or sickness caused by AI use.

The AI needs to consider the number of tasks allocated to each employee, their difficulty and how long each task will take. 'Otherwise, the risk is that some employees become overworked while other employees are underworked, which could lead to ill-health in either scenario,' says Hübner.

To prevent mismatch of work requires that the AI is trained using adequate data and that humans (including workers, their line managers and even Occupational Health physicians) are involved in decision-making.

Ida Nordmark, an associate at Delphi, says organisations could face fines and damages claims for employee injury or sickness caused by AI use.

For example, under Swedish labour law a company that causes ill health or injury in an employee because of it using AI is responsible for bearing the costs of his/her rehabilitation. In more serious cases, a company may be fined by the regulator for causing an employee's illness in the workplace or be required to pay damages due to discrimination. 'The most obvious risk is not legal, but reputational,' says Nordmark.

This is the scene in some parts of Europe.

India does not have specific laws for data protection but personal information is safeguarded under Section 43A and Section 72A of The Information Technology Act. It gives a right to compensation for improper disclosure of personal information similar to GDPR (General Data Protection Regulation). In 2017, the Supreme Court of India declared the Right to privacy as a Fundamental Right protected under the Indian Constitution.

However, unlike the European governments, the Indian government and many other governments aren't even thinking of effect of AI on worker health and the compensation involved therein.

AI improves safety but can create unsafe work parameters of working, due to lack of 'prevention through design' approach including automatic algorithm system, leading to work-related (occupational) illnesses and accidents.

26

Robots at workplace and mental health

(published on 25th July, 2023 in www.occupationist.com)

Robots are already in use – in offices and factories, in affluent homes, in hospitals etc. They are useful for certain types of jobs. Robots are being made to do more intricate jobs in future.

How do workers view the presence of robots at workplace working alongside them?

The reactions are varied.

A toy-like robot can promote mental wellbeing in the workplace.

To some, the presence of robots is fun, while for others it is a source of fear. And it depends from country to country as you will read below.

According to a study by the University of Cambridge presented in March 2023 at the ACM/IEEE International Conference on Human-Robot interaction held in Stockholm, interacting with a toy-like robot can promote mental wellbeing in the workplace.

The results suggest that robots can be a useful tool for promoting workplace wellbeing, as employees reported feeling more relaxed and less stressed after a 4-week program on wellness. The facial expressions of the robots were also found to be effective in helping to create a more positive workplace atmosphere.

However, the scene is totally different in the US.

> ***To some, the robots the presence of robots is fun, while for others it is a source of fear. And it depends from country to country due to labor laws.***

In the US, the presence of robots in the workplace is causing mental health issues in workers who experience heightened levels of distress and even turned to substance abuse, reported Osea Giuntella and his team of scientists in the 2022 study.

Osea Giuntella, who is the author of the study and an assistant professor of economics at the University of Pittsburgh explained, 'Robots are good for physical health – they usually take on jobs that are physically intensive and may even hurt you. But in the U.S., there's this understanding that the robots may take your job because there's a less protective labor market.'

The problem is uniquely American.

Giuntella says, 'In Germany, the introduction of robots was not related to job displacement. Instead, new and young workers were brought to other sectors of the industry, while the job security of incumbent workers was not affected.' He notes, 'German workers were better protected in their work from German robots.' Unfortunately, the US companies offer few of the same protections, which experts says leads to feelings of job insecurity.

And job security leads to stress, which in turn leads to substance abuse, lowered productivity and even higher suicide rates.

'Perception is reality,' says Mindy Shoss, an associate professor of psychology at the University of Central Florida, in Orlando, who has been studying the impacts of robot integration in labor markets for years. 'In our papers, we try to make the point that technology is not predetermined, but how people react to it determines how technology is adopted into the workplace and whether or not it succeeds.'

Involving Occupational Health (OH) physicians at an early project stage whenever new technologies are introduced will help them anticipate health related issues, plan mitigation measures and advise the senior management accordingly. This will reassure the workers.

Shoss, who was not involved with the new study, added that the findings raised important questions about differences in the introduction of these new technologies, depending on the country. She pointed out that when workers are first being introduced to their robotic co-workers, it is critical to help people understand their shifting roles in the workplace, and how to make the best of the incorporation of these new 'workers.'

When new technologies at workplace are not understood, the workers, especially the American workers fear that a new robot by their side could mean threat to their job. This is because America has less protective labor market.

'For that reason, companies, managers, technology developers, government, all need to pay attention to a variety of outcomes, including health, safety, well-being and profits – some of those more traditional considerations – when it comes to these technologies,' Shoss said.

Joblessness creates lawlessness and is a major threat to law makers as their political fortunes are defined by the jobs they create rather than robots they generate.

Not just robots, but while introducing any other technology, it is very important to take the existing workers into confidence and choose the technology after the workers have understood its implications. Worker-friendly labor laws of the country in which technology is being introduced also helps.

MIT (Massachusetts Institute of Technology, USA) researchers are working on social interactions of robots between themselves. When videos of these social interactions between robots were shown to human beings, they agreed that robots are learning it well. This worsens the fear in employees even more leading to even more stress at workplace as now the robots will have the requisite social skills.

Industry leaders should take a cue from the research and also involve Occupational Health (OH) physicians whenever new technologies are introduced. Involving the OH physician proactively at the early project stage while introducing new technologies will lead to anticipating health related issues arising due to use of new technologies, plan mitigation measures and advise the senior management accordingly. This will also reassure employees, avoid conflicts and save company's time. The role of the OH physician is not reactive. Management not supporting proactive role of an OH physician will result in the company dealing with large numbers of employees having stress, substance abuse and other mental health issues due to introduction of new technologies, which will impact productivity.

And of course, the local labor laws should support workers over machines! Joblessness creates lawlessness and is a major threat to law makers as their political fortunes are defined by the jobs they create rather than robots they generate. More robots means more lawlessness which in turn translates to a bleak political future of the politicians.

———————

27

Managing your mental health is mostly about 'having a frank timely talk'

(published on 7th June, 2023 in www.occupationist.com)

What do you do when you feel low? I asked this to a few of my close friends and acquaintances. The answers I got varied from, 'I eat sugar,' 'go for a drink to a pub alone even if a friend is not available to give company,' and 'talk to a friend'.

All three actions help when you are low, as revealed by the respondents.

There is no one method to overcome the feeling of being low. But one easy method is to talk frankly to somebody, preferably a friend. Talking gives you a new high; talking in time when feeling 'low' in life takes you higher. Hence, I often say, 'everyone should have at least one trusted friend.'

Recently, two examples have been reported in the lay press. One is about Kapil Sharma, a famous Indian standup comedian on what he did when he was not just low but was going through depression. And the other is about Rohit Sharma, the Indian cricketer.

Talking gives you a new high; talking in time when feeling 'low' in life takes you higher.

Deepika Padukone, a leading Indian actress has been talking about depression for a while. In the past Amitabh Bachchan, Shah Rukh Khan, Rajesh Khanna, Dilip Kumar, Sanjay Dutt (all Indian film actors) have all gone into depression in their lives. Some bounced back better than before, some bounce back reasonably well but some just couldn't.

These few examples show that mental health issues can affect anyone and steps should be taken in time either by the person undergoing the 'low' or can be proactively taken by a well-meaning friend.

Delaying the talk with someone when feeling 'low' will push you faster and deeper into the blackhole of depression.

In case of Kapil Sharma, it was Shah Rukh Khan (SRK), a leading India film actor who came to his rescue. While in case of Rohit Sharma, it was Yuvraj Singh, a famed Indian cricketer.

Kapil Sharma had developed a dubious reputation of cancelling or delaying shoots. He was at that time fighting with alcoholism which contributed to his anxiety and depression. He once cancelled a shoot at the last moment with Shah Rukh Khan.

Kapil told in an interview for a popular talk show in AajTak, that 3-4 days after he had the shoot cancelled with SRK, they met in the same studio. Kapil says, SRK understood what was happening, so he called him to his car and sat with him for an hour. According to Kapil, SRK asked him if he took drugs, to which he replied no. But Kapil told SRK that 'I no longer feel like working.' Kapil further said that SRK told him 'some very nice things and counselled me.'

And it worked. Kapil is back with a bang on TV. It shows how things can change for good when two people have a frank talk.

The best EAP (Employee Assistance Program) is not always a third-party counsellor but can be your best friend or even a trusted colleague.

In case of Rohit Sharma, he felt depressed for about a month when he was unable to secure a spot despite past successes in 15-member Indian cricket team. Rohit Sharma recently told Jemimah Rodrigues, an Indian woman cricketer, of the time when he was dropped from the Indian team. He said he was depressed for a month. There was only one person, Yuvraj Singh, who came up to him, took him out for dinner and there was nobody else.

Jemimah also shared the invaluable advice that Rohit Sharma gave her, which ultimately led to her successful return to the Indian women's team. The advice Rohit gave was, 'tough times will happen but you know it is what you do next. Make sure when you get the next opportunity, you are ready for it. It happens or doesn't happen, its fine.'

So, whenever you think you have mental health issues, just talk and chances are everything will be fine. The sooner you talk, the better and faster is the outcome. Else, sometimes, depression lingers on and can play havoc with life.

In my talks on depression, I emphasize on the importance of 'having a talk' whenever one feels 'low' for more than 2-3 days. Delaying the talk when feeling 'low' will push you faster and deeper into the blackhole of depression. Not having a talk with someone in time will prolong the misery of the mental health issues.

In factories and offices which employ doctors (especially if they are qualified Occupational Health physicians), they should encourage the culture of having frank talks in case of mental health issues. The best EAP (Employee Assistance Program) is not always a third-party counsellor but can be your best friend or even a trusted colleague.

Gig economy and worker health

(published on 31st May, 2023 in www.occupationist.com)

Gig work is temporary or freelance work performed by a person independently on an informal or on-demand basis. Gig work consists of income-earning activities that do not have long-term employer-employee relationship.

Gig economy is the contribution of these workers to the economy of the businesses they work in as well as to the overall economy of the countries in which they work.

> ***Gig workers are a vulnerable group. Gig work can be dangerous.***

In the US, it is estimated that 55 million Americans work in the gig economy. McKinsey Global Institute and other reputed agencies estimate that between 25 and 35 percent of workers are engaged in gig work on a supplementary or primary basis. About 10 percent of workers are engaged in gig work as their main job. Less than 1 percent are with online platforms (like Uber, TaskRabbit etc.), also called as platform workers.

In India, there are no estimates regarding the number of gig workers but looking at the success of online platforms (Zomato, Delhivery, Swiggy etc.) the numbers must be bigger than in USA. However, The Code on Social Security 2020 which was passed in Parliament in September 2020 provides for social security for gig and platform workers along with unorganised sector workers.

This is a great initiative by the PM Narendra Modi's government wherein gig and platform workers have been defined and incorporated within the ambit of labour laws. As it is happening for the first time there are issues about overlapping definitions and how to make the registration more inclusive.

Work content and working conditions of gig workers being ill-defined (non-standard work), they sometimes end up running errands for their employers.

Gig and platform worker is a new name for workers doing certain types of jobs but essentially, they are a subset of a larger set of unorganised sector workers. Hence keeping three separate categories – unorganised, gig and platform workers – is not really necessary due to overlaps.

Although the Code on Social Security 2020 defines workers for sake of wages and compensation issues, it does not make any provision about their work and working conditions and its impact on health.

Similarly, there are safety issues as platform workers as they visit unfamiliar homes and offices to deliver parcels.

Even in the US, these challenges look scary without appropriate occupational health regulations and enforcement.

Gig worker should be treated no differently than other employees. The risks peculiar to their work should be assessed and efforts done to mitigate them.

Work content and working conditions of gig workers being ill-defined (non-standard work), they sometimes end up running errands for their employers. Generally, there are no classifications in gig workers – intellectual vs manual work, blue-collar vs white collar or services vs goods. This situation is worse off than workers in unorganised sectors like construction workers, fishing, agriculture etc. where there is some classification and generic health advices can be implemented.

Gig workers are a vulnerable group. Gig work can be dangerous – as even in the western nations a gig worker does work without much training regarding the job, is low paid, is temporary, without health or retiring benefits, and unsafe. It lacks career training, promotion opportunities and collective bargaining.

Neo liberalization of economy has increased work and health-related precarization (dangers) and led to a social class of people those who have no job security or prospect of regular employment.

Since gig work is an occupation, albeit relatively new in this age of neoliberalism, and the number of gig workers are likely to increase by millions in every country in the next few years, the contribution of Occupational Health associations and physicians will be of utmost importance.

Ideally, gig worker should be treated no differently than other employees. The risks peculiar to their work should be assessed and efforts done to mitigate them.

Typical risks of gig workers are job insecurity leading to stress; low wages (or fluctuating incomes) leading to poor sleep quality, headaches and backaches; excessive driving leading to higher cardio-vascular risks; working in hot weather conditions leading to dehydration, heat exhaustion, heat stroke etc.

Interestingly, in India, the Occupational Safety, Health and Workplace Conditions Code mandates companies to create safe working conditions for employees but does not include any provisions for outdoor workers working in harsh climatic conditions.

Gig work is here to stay – it will transform the future of work globally; hence, it is necessary that businesses employing them demonstrate taking care of their working conditions as that impacts health, both short-term and long-term.

Neo liberalization of economy has increased work and health related precarization (dangers) and led to a social class of people those who have no job security or prospect of regular employment.

Since gig work is an occupation, albeit relatively new in this age of neoliberalism, and the number of gig workers are likely to increase by millions in every country in the next few years, the contribution of Occupational Health associations and physicians will be of utmost importance.

Globally, the OH associations and physicians must influence the governments in the countries they reside to introduce legislation and create work standards that are conducive to both the businesses and the gig workers alike with special attention to working conditions and worker health.

Amongst the business owners and corporations, the OH associations must strive to create awareness in them, influence compassion and generate the willingness to take action about health and wellbeing of all workers, including gig workers.

End of Covid pandemic is not an end to good habits it taught

(published on 20ᵗʰ May, 2023 in www.occupationist.com)

On Friday, 5ᵗʰ May 2023, the WHO (World Health Organization) declared the end of pandemic. The WHO on 11ᵗʰ March 2020 had declared the Covid-19 outbreak a global pandemic. Prior to this WHO had declared on 30ᵗʰ January 2020 the ongoing spread of infections as Public Health Emergency of International Concern (PHEIC).

The word pandemic has all the words that are in panic.

As early as 23ʳᵈ January 2020, I had issued a health alert company-wide via an email. I had talked about it informally to many about a possible global spread.

It was perhaps the first ever health advisory on Covid sent to a select community in India. This was on the basis that it had spread to many countries, China is not very far away from India, increased international travel can cause infections to spread rapidly and the US CDC on 1ˢᵗ January 2020 identified that a wet animal market was responsible for the outbreak.

The text of the advisory sent is in italics below.

Health alert: Wuhan virus - 2019 novel coronavirus (nCoV)

23 January 2020

Dear colleagues

A new virus (2019 novel coronavirus – 2019 nCoV) that seems to have originated from infected animals at a seafood market in the Wuhan district of China is causing respiratory illness, pneumonia and death in some instances. Around 574 people in China and six abroad have been diagnosed with infection of which 17 have died.

The entire city of Wuhan has been quarantined. Airports and railway stations in Wuhan have been temporarily closed. Isolated cases have been reported from USA, Taiwan, South Korea, Japan and Thailand. No case has been identified in India however, thermal screening of passengers at the international airports in many countries including India and USA has commenced.

World Health Organization (WHO) has not yet declared the Wuhan virus as a 'public health emergency of international concern.'

As human-to-human transmission is possible the following actions are recommended:

- *Do not visit wet markets or farms*
- *Keep distance from people who are sick*
- *Maintain good personal hygiene*
- *Wash your hands often with soap and water for at least 20 seconds and*
- *use an alcohol-based hand sanitizer if soap and water are not available.*
- *Carry hand sanitiser for use when soap and water are not readily available.*

- *Avoid touching your face*
- *Avoid direct contact with animals (live or dead) and their environment. Do*
- *not touch surfaces that may be contaminated with droppings.*
- *Ensure food, including eggs and meat are thoroughly cooked*

Seek medical attention if you develop symptoms, especially fever or shortness of breath. Do not travel if you are sick as many countries have implemented screening, and travelers may face quarantine and testing.

On 20th January 2020, China had announced 200 infected cases with 3 deaths. By 22nd January, the number of cases in China had more than doubled at 500 with 17 deaths. This was enough to unleash panic.

The word pandemic has all the words that are in panic. Is the pandemic around, I thought, and wanted to alert people in my influence – by a health advisory to employees and verbally to known people. Some were upset that I was over-reacting and creating fear!

On 27th January 2020, I attended a 4-day international conference on Occupational Health in Mumbai where discussion around Covid did take place.

The learnings from Covid are evergreen. They are the writing on the wall. Following them on a continual basis will allow us to manage a lot of diseases, including infectious diseases like the seasonal influenza and milder forms of Covid in future.

The declaration of end of pandemic does not mean end of good habits that pandemic taught. Covid is still killing. As I write, Covid continues to kill one person every 5 minutes somewhere in the world – that is about 100,000 people annually. The threat of pandemic like situation remains.

In developing countries, including India, it is still necessary to use a mask as it is a barrier to the dust in the air. The dust contains a lot of allergens, pollens and spores of diseases causing germs.

I continue to use mask whenever I visit a hospital or sit in an autorickshaw in Mumbai to commute and feel happy when I see some autorickshaw drivers continuing to use the mask.

Everyone should be mindful of the good habits learnt during the pandemic and must continue to follow them to prevent from getting sick personally and to prevent a pandemic like situation to erupt again.

Pandemic taught us to wash hands the correct way. Never be in a hurry to wash hands. Improperly washed hands can lead to self-infestation as well as cause a lot of diseases in self and others.

Business owners, public health experts, Occupational Health physicians, NGOs, schools and colleges and other public figures should continue to engage the population to remind them of the good habits and follow them regularly just as they did during the pandemic.

A pandemic may strike again - we do not know when, we have no idea about its nature or intensity. But in an over- populous, highly competitive world, organizing a pandemic and creating disruption is far more easier than using military. Individuals and governments should be aware of this possibility and be ready to tackle it. The Covid pandemic experience will help, both the individuals and the governments! As an Occupational Health (OH) physician working in an industry, keeping the workers in a state of healthcare readiness will help them improve their selfcare.

———————

30

Carbon Monoxide: a dangerous gas in homes, offices & factories

(published on 30th April, 2023 in www.occupationist.com)

Presence of carbon monoxide (CM) can cause irritating symptoms and even death depending on its concentration in the ambient air. CM is present not just in factories and offices but in homes too.

Basement car parking spaces are also a source where carbon monoxide (CM) levels can develop to annoying if not fatal levels.

As per CDC (Centers for Disease Control and Prevention), each year more than 400 people in America die from unintentional CM poisoning. CM poisoning leads to approximately 50,000 visits to the Casualty (Emergency Room) and around 4000 hospitalizations. In UK around 4000 people make a visit to the Casualty for unintentional CM poisoning.

CM poisoning is associated with health effects. At low concentrations, CM causes fatigue in healthy people and chest pain in those with heart diseases. At moderate concentrations it causes impaired vision, angina and reduced brain function. At high concentrations, it is known to cause dizziness, headache, confusion, nausea, flu-like symptoms that clears up after leaving the place and fatality (at very high concentration).

The best way of preventing carbon monoxide (CM) from entering the office is by ensuring a visit by a professional engineer to service the heating appliances annually.

To measure CM levels, devices are available. The current OSHA PEL (Occupational Safety and Health Administration Permissible Exposure Limit) for CM is 50 ppm as an 8-hour time weighted average.

Average CM levels in homes without gas stoves vary from 0.5 to 5 parts per million (ppm); near properly adjusted gas stoves are between 5 to 15 ppm and near poorly adjusted stoves are 30 ppm or higher. Many people in colder areas of developing countries are found dead as they inhale CM when they burn coal overnight to keep themselves warm in their poorly ventilated houses.

In offices, the source of CM is heating of office space during winter months. If the heating appliance using fossil fuels or wood are badly maintained or installed, they may not burn the fuel efficiently or vent correctly resulting in production of CM.

The best way of preventing CM from entering the office is by ensuring a visit by a professional engineer to service the heating appliances annually. They will check their condition, and advise on any repairs necessary for its proper functioning.

Source of carbon monoxide (CM) in homes is either a firepot or an electric room heater.

In factories, CM pollution results from incomplete burning of material containing carbon such as kerosene, coal, wood, natural gas, petrol, diesel etc. Forges, blast furnaces and coke ovens produce CM but the most common source of exposure is the internal combustion engine.

Basement car parking spaces are also a source where CM levels can develop to annoying if not fatal levels. Hence it is good to instal CM sensors, exhaust fans and advise chauffeurs and other car owners to refrain from keeping the engine running or waiting in the basement for long hours.

A CM sensor can be programmed to alert if the level of CM exceeds the permitted level of ppm. If the sensors detect that the level of CM has exceeded the permitted levels, exhaust fans are switched on. The air contaminated with CM is removed from the area and brings fresh air. A Variable Frequency Drive (VFD) controls the speed of the exhaust fans based on the ppm level.

In a 2017 study from AIIMS, New Delhi involving 40 cases of fatal CM poisoning it was found that 80% of cases were reported in winter months. 39 of them died with a source of CM nearby and the person was inside the room or some closed space without ventilation. In most cases, the source of CM was either a firepot or an electric room heater. Some cases of CM build inside the car with a running engine.

Occupations affected by CM poisoning include custom inspector, Diesel engine operator, firefighter, forklift operator, garage mechanic, police officer, taxi driver, toll booth attendant, welder, marine terminal worker etc.

Steps to reduce exposure to CM that individuals and business owners must understand include:

- Educate workers how to identify presence of CM and about the risks of exposure
- Provide personal CM monitors having audible alarms to employees who are at risk
- Gas appliances should be properly adjusted
- Having a vented heater helps
- In kerosene heaters use proper fuel
- 'On' the exhaust fans while using gas stoves
- Open the flue (a pipe) of a fireplace is in use

- Use electricity or battery powered equipment instead of gasoline-powered machines
- Get all central-heating systems (furnaces, flues, chimneys etc.) inspected annually by a professional and repair any leaks without delay
- Do not keep the car engine ON in a garage, basement car parks or in a poorly ventilated place
- Install battery-operated detectors that measure accumulation of CM over time and have audible alarms. When the CM levels get too high, the detector sounds an alarm, allowing workers to evacuate or ventilate the area
- Test the air on a regular basis in areas where CM is expected to be present

As a temporary measure, additional ventilation can be used for short periods of time when high levels of CM are anticipated.

Report for immediate action by workers working with heating equipment if they notice:

- Gas flames that burn orange or yellow instead of blue
- Soot marks on or above the field-fired appliance
- Coal or wood fires that do not stay lit
- Increased condensation inside the windows
- Fire that is difficult to ignite
- Boiler making a banging or clanking noise
- The pilot light on the boiler keeps going out
- The chimney or flue is blocked
- A musty smell

CM is colorless and odorless and hence is difficult to detect.

First Aid: If it appears that a worker has been exposed to high levels of CM, the following steps taken immediately can save a life:

- Move the worker outdoors to a place where there is fresh air
- Call Ambulance
- If the worker is breathing, first-aiders should administer 100 percent oxygen
- If the worker is not breathing, first-aiders should administer CPR (Cardio Pulmonary Resuscitation)

The role of Occupational Health (OH) Physician is to create awareness about CM poisoning in business operations and along with Industrial Hygienist make sure that steps are taken to monitor CM levels and CM alarms are installed at appropriate places. The OH physician should develop a robust training program for employees to identify CM poisoning and provide first-aiders (trained in CPR, oxygen administration etc.) as necessary. Provision of an ACLS ambulance and a tie-up with a tertiary care hospital having hyperbaric chamber will help persons with severe CM poisoning. Severe CM poisoning requires placing the person in a high-pressure (hyperbaric) chamber and breathe 100% oxygen.

31

Toxic positivity at workplace

(published on 27th April, 2023 in www.occupationist.com)

On 3rd March 2023, Times of India, a newspaper, flashed a news with a heading *'Toxic body positivity: Ranbir Kapoor says actors are starved, unhappy, and pained, do not eat enough.'* Ranbir Kapoor is a young popular actor in Indian cinema. He spoke about this during an event to promote his film 'Tu Jhooti Main Makkar.'

A thought immediately passed my mind. What about the common man. And what about millions of workers all over the world. Aren't they also victims of toxic positivity in one way or the other, at workplace and elsewhere. And what can be done about it.

Toxic positivity is forced cheerfulness that can lead to mental health problems, including burnout.

Ranbir Kapoor went on to say that actors today are unhappy and pained because they starve themselves to look in a certain way. The pressure to look glamourous and cool on actors makes them fake their emotions when in reality they are unhappy.

If the pressure to behave or look in a certain way continues unabated, it can lead to mental health problems, including burnout. And toxic positivity is all about that. It is forced cheerfulness.

The actors are answerable to the public. They can do little about it. For the actors and the public alike, toxic positivity (TP) is an occupational hazard that must be mitigated to ALARP (as low as reasonably practicable) so that harm to body and mind is minimal.

Toxic Positivity has givers and receivers. The givers must realize that they are creating a workplace that will eventually engulf them as well. Hence, each one of us should refrain from remarks that propagate toxic positivity.

Comments such as 'good vibes only' or 'you are bringing everyone down' or 'chin up' at workplace when you are having a bad day is an experience of toxic positivity.

Incidentally, TP comes from a well-meaning source and is usually unintended but can have disastrous consequences for the worker in a workplace.

In TP, there are givers who create the culture and there are receivers who get immediately affected. The givers must realize that they are creating a place that will eventually become negative and engulf them as well. Hence each one of us should refrain from remarks that propagate TP.

Creating an awareness about toxic positivity can be a wellness initiative for all employees including leaders because if left uncontrolled can lead to stress and other mental health problems.

If a business has to succeed, everyone in the workplace, right from top to bottom should be mindful of toxic positivity and refrain from comments that invalidate negative emotions in their colleagues.

This pressure to show only 'good side of yourself' can backfire, making people feel less safe, less positive, less connected, less resilient; eventually damaging the workforce morale and the business.

Creating an awareness about toxic positivity can be a wellness initiative because if left uncontrolled can lead to stress and other mental health problems. It should involve everyone including the leaders.

Being positive is not toxic, but suppressing an emotion or getting a demoralising response makes it toxic. If TP at workplace is not recognised and addressed, it can lead to trauma, isolation and unhealthy coping mechanism in a lot of employees that will be detrimental for the business.

Even if optimism is a great idea, one cannot be forever happy. At workplace, many people feel they have to be happy as it is the expectation of the surrounding. If you realize that you are expected to hide your true emotions and be positive all the time even if you are not, then it is time to learn to manage the expectation urgently.

One should feel the negative emotions instead of suppressing them. When you suppress negative emotions instead of feeling them because it is an expectation of your family, friends, colleagues or seniors to be positive all the time, you are in a state of toxic positivity.

Positivity is beneficial to health and mental well-being; toxic positivity is detrimental.

The reason why workplaces give so much importance to positivity that it becomes toxic has a historical story. However, we will not go into the history. Instead, focus on how to manage toxic positivity.

Since toxic positivity is stressful and eventually leads to burnout, inputs from an Occupational Health (OH) physician should help. While managing mental health, it is important to talk about toxic positivity and the senior management should be sensitised about it.

The fact is that in this mad world of social media, everyone faces toxic positivity because we fall prey to the expectation of others. One who sets the expectation and creates TP is the giver while the recipient is to whom it is intended. The environment of TP can be subtle or outrageous depending on circumstances.

TP is an expectation initiated by someone to a recipient who becomes a victim. The victim is expected to always stay positive and hide negative feelings which leads to stress. In a workplace setting, the senior management or the supervisor should avoid initiating an expectation of being forever positive and the recipient should resist from being affected. This is possible only when both the initiator of TP and its recipient understand that it is good to be positive but expecting too much positivity always is not possible as everyone has a bad day.

Five signs of TP:

- Feeling guilty for getting angry or upset on others
- Hiding true feeling
- Scolding people who are not positive
- Invalidating emotions of others
- Dismissal of all feeling that are negative

Just imagine if this was a workplace culture. How stifled and tense would you feel. Eventually such a workplace will lead to burnout in most of the workers.

How does toxic positivity harm:

- Can lead to feelings of shame
- Can also cause feelings of guilt
- It avoids real human emotion
- Increases stress
- Reduces well-being

- Delays or halts progress in life, generally

How can you cope with toxic positivity:

- Being realistic
- Challenge the person who incites toxic positivity
- Do not hesitate to speak to your coach, mentor or therapist
- Encourage others to express feelings
- Have empathy for others
- Solve the problem rather than ignore it
- Be aware that it is normal to have occasional negative emotions

What business owners can do:

- Create safe and comfortable spaces
- Be honest and transparent
- Make well-being a priority
- Sensitize the employees, managers and leaders to understand implications of toxic positivity

Positivity is beneficial to health and mental well-being; toxic positivity is detrimental. Toxic positivity at workplace has to be dealt at multiple levels of hierarchy as organizations are seldom flat.

Kharghar heatwave deaths: seek Occupational Health advice too!

(appeared on 19th April, 2023 in www.occupationist.com)

Sunday, 16th April 2023 was a deadly day for 14 people who had come to attend a social rally to be addressed by A-list politicians in Kharghar, a suburb in Navi Mumbai, India.

As they came to attend a socio-political rally, 14 of them were dead and many were in hospital being treated for sunstroke, a medical condition that occurs after getting dehydrated in the intense sun for long hours.

The occasion at Kharghar was an award ceremony that was expecting around 1 million (ten lakh) people to attend. The timing was beginning of the Indian summer. The arrangements seemed to be ill-planned even though the budget of the event was approx. 1.7 million US dollars (Rs. 14 crores). As per a newspaper report, 14 people lost their life, mostly women.

Plans remain on paper if there is no awareness or an informed, enthusiastic executioner.

Rallies will continue to happen, not only in India but all over the globe. Should the people attending have to die? What can be done to prevent such incidents from happening again.

Wherever the word prevent is uttered, a much less medical specialty by the name Occupational Health (OH) is the most useful but seldom considered by authorities or rally organizers. That is simply because of lack of awareness.

Most countries have a National Disaster Plan. If followed many of these kinds of tragedies can be averted. After all, deaths during a socio-political or a political rally is not the aim of the organisers as it can defame the A-list politicians who were present or anyone for that matter.

Attending a rally is not an occupation, yet principles of OH can be applied to any situation where health can be proactively protected and an illness prevented. This is what makes OH all pervasive.

Plans remain on paper if there is no awareness or an informed, enthusiastic executioner.

For example, medical specialist who deals with worker health (the Occupational Health physicians) take care of the workers working out in the sun by making sure at least the following is done:

- Sensitize the senior management about effect of heat on health, safety and performance
- Ensure senior management sensitizes the site managers
- Conduct separate sessions on effects of heat for site managers and workers expected to be supervising or working out in the sun
- Have shade areas for workers to rest for 10 minutes after 45 to 60 minutes of working in the sun or hot areas
- Provide clean and cool potable water and encourage workers to drink during the 10-minute break
- Provide ablution facilities as otherwise workers avoid drinking enough water which in turn leads to dehydration

- Maintain high level of preparedness to deal with any heat-related health effects (keep ambulance(s) close by)

In a rally, the organizers must be sensitized about the health effects on people due to being out in the sun. They should be aware of the national/regional advisory on heatwave. And they should seek OH advice as the OH physicians have hands-on experience of handling workers working out in the sun.

Attending a rally is not an occupation, yet principles of OH can be applied to any situation where health can be proactively protected and an illness prevented. This is what makes OH all pervasive. It has immense usefulness wherever harm to health or life can be prevented, Kharghar rally was one of them.

It is time the governments should consider seeking OH inputs to avert such tragedies.

The awareness to proactive or preventive care is so low that it is time that the local media responsibly sensitize the organizers of rallies.

Ideally, arrangements to have overhead shade, clean and cool potable water, washrooms etc. must be a part of the rally, whatever the numbers. The audience were out in the sun for around 6 hours without water; while some were camping overnight.

Of the many lessons to be learnt after the Kharghar tragedy, one is to seek Occupational Health advice for at least one reason – that it prevents proactively.

If socio-political or political rallies must be successful it is important that the lessons learnt be implemented with immediate effect else avertable hardships and tragedies will continue leading to a questionable future of such rallies.

Of the many lessons to be learnt after the Kharghar tragedy, one is to seek Occupational Health advice for at least one reason – that it prevents illnesses proactively. The Kharghar tragedy was preventable.

All women Work:
A brief history of work and their health

(published on 8th March, 2023 in www.occupationist.com)

All women work, including the full-time homemakers. How does the work (job) impact women and their health?

Women have been working since time immemorial, mostly at home doing all the household work. In the olden days it was common to have 5 or more children on an average. Looking after the needs of these children as well as the husband was like running a small office of 6 people today. All jobs were done single-handedly and were time-bound, as the husband had to leave for work in time and the kids to school. She was and is a supply chain expert as she continues to make available all supplies for smooth running of the house. All this causes stress.

Women leaving a job due to health reasons in the 21st century is unacceptable.

Women's work has not always been accurately recorded in history. This is due to much of women's work being irregular, home-based or in family-run businesses. Census done in the early years of 19th century often show a blank space under the 'occupation' column against women's names. There is some evidence that from 1850 onwards women were engaged in wide variety of work that paid them wages in the UK.

The stress increased when women were forced to enter the workforce to provide secondary income for the family needs. The household work (cooking, cleaning, child care, having an animal like cow, growing vegetable in the backyard etc.) that was unpaid also had to be completed. This added even more stress.

The working conditions in general were horrific and the women worked in factories, mines, textile mills, farms or as domestic service for the rich and were paid less than men. Few women worked from home in occupations such as laundry, finishing garments and shoes for factories or preparation of snacks to sell in the market.

A woman was and is a supply chain expert as she continues to make available all supplies for smooth running of the house.

There were factories coming up as a part of Industrial Revolution which was the time (1760 AD to 1840 AD) when the shift to new manufacturing processes occurred in the Great Britain which soon spread to France and the United States of America.

During Industrial Revolution, more working hands were required and women were employed as their wages were one-third to one-half of a man's average salary. Soon the children, as young as 6 years old, joined in as their wages were even lower.

Women would work during the Industrial Revolution for 11 hours with a 45-minute break and if they broke rule they would be strapped. They worked in dangerous environments with dust covering from head to toe. There were no masks or any safety equipment. Food offered was poor and often covered with dust and hence inedible.

Tough working conditions continued till 1930s. In fact, during an exceptionally cold July of 1888, one of the most famous strikes by women workers occurred at the Byrant and May match factory in the East End of London when 200 workers left work in protest because the factory owners sacked three workers who had talked to Annie Besant, a social reformer, about their working conditions.

Yes, she is the same Annie Besant who was involved with politics in India and helped launch the Home Rule League to campaign for democracy in India in 1914. This led her to become the President of Indian National Congress in 1917.

An article was published by Besant in her halfpenny weekly paper 'The Link' on 23rd June 1888 titled 'White Slavery in London'. The article was about working conditions at the Byrant and May factory highlighting poor pay, 14-hour work days, excessive fines and health problems arising from working with white phosphorus.

Women would work during the Industrial Revolution for 11 hours with a 45-minute break and if they broke rule they would be strapped.

It is ironic that around the same time, Jamsetji Tata of the Tata Group in India opened one of its very first enterprises, the Empress Mills at Nagpur, on 1st January 1877. The Empress Mills established two creches for babies of the women who were employed there. Girls who worked half-time in the mill could attend classes in reading, writing and needlework. A primary school was also established. For older children, two factory schools were established. By 1921, maternity benefit allowance was available to women who were employed for 11 months or more to be given two months paid maternity benefit. This was perhaps the first housing colony for workers in the world!

The Empress Mills went on to establish 7 night-schools where languages, music and dance were taught. Four gyms were set up for exercise and good health and sports made an integral part of life at the Empress Mills. Employees had free medical facilities. A Health Week was organized each year to highlight various diseases and how workers could keep themselves and families safe. This was perhaps the first example globally of Occupational Health in practice, albeit, unknowingly that it is a medical specialty devoted to worker health.

Empress Mills established Provident Fund (PF) in 1901, decades before it was legally mandated. An accident compensation scheme was established in 1895 and a Pension Fund in 1887. Last but not the least, to further help the workers, a cooperative credit society was also set up around the same time.

While opening an extension of Empress Mills in 1895, Jamsetji Tata said, 'We do not claim to be more unselfish, more generous or more philanthropic than other people. But, we think, we started on sound and straightforward business principles, considering the interests of our shareholders our own, and the health and welfare of our employees the sure foundation of our prosperity'.

In the first half of 20th century (1930 onwards), many Acts and Laws were passed by various governments, including India, where issues like minimum wages, working conditions, compensation etc. were addressed.

In 1877, Jamsetji Tata established schools, creches, gyms etc. in Empress Mills. Medical facilities were free and health week was observed every year.

After the famous strike by women workers at Byrant and May match factory in London, the workers took their campaign to the parliament and with the support of London Trades Council, all their demands were met, eventually leading to formation of a Union of Women Match Workers.

Women continued their pursuit to work, and most of them in unorganized sectors in developing countries, still are with wages far below men, despite having laws.

Health issues in women are more than in men due to multiple reasons – not taking care of themselves being the foremost – the sacrifice for family is paramount in most cultures across the world.

If women do not take care of themselves, soon they will equal men in diseases that earlier weren't theirs.

Women, on this International Women's Day (2023), take a pledge to have a work-life balance. Only if you take care of yourself can you take care of the family and job. Work-life balance is for women too. The men should share home responsibilities as well to allow time for women to have work-life balance. Where possible, the 60:40 'work from home' rule is a nice way that employers can indirectly encourage work-life balance amongst their workers.

Imbalance in work-life balance causes stress which in turn causes a lot of illnesses. Women who were not prone to some diseases earlier are prone to those as they enter the workforce, both organized and unorganized. If they do not take care of themselves, soon they will equal men in diseases that earlier weren't theirs.

In India, according to one estimate, it is said that 86% of working women have seen their colleagues, relatives or friends drop out of the workforce, of which 59% due to health issues as the main reason.

Women leaving a job due to health reasons in the 21st century is unacceptable. The sooner we investigate and find solutions the better. Access to Occupational Health physician makes it easier to seek inputs to mitigate specifically any health effects due to work in women and any other concern so that drop out of the workforce be reduced.

However, no one can make the workplace conducive to their health and contribute to change the work scenario except the women themselves!

Making workplace disability-friendly

(published on 12th February, 2023 in www.occupationist.com)

If you have arthritis, a bone joint disability, or any other medical condition that restricts your mobility (movements), and if your workplace is safe for you, it is disability-friendly.

Is your workplace designed to make you move freely so that the chances of your tripping and falling are minimized to ALARP (as low as reasonably practicable). Can a worker on a wheelchair come to the workplace? If yes, your workplace is disability-friendly.

There could be employees who have medical conditions that limit their mobility and not having the workplace designed to make them comfortable signals poor ergonomics and a disregard to employees' concerns.

There are many other things, some ergonomics as well, that go into making workers comfortable at work, more so for the worker with mobility issues.

Even if there is just one worker, modifications should be made. In fact, workplaces should be such that just anyone, disability or not, must be able to work without fear of developing a work-related illness or getting injured due to trips and falls due to the environment in which he/she works.

There could be employees who have medical conditions that limit their mobility and not having the workplace designed to make them comfortable signals poor ergonomics and a disregard to employees' concerns.

Disability can happen to anyone – a worker today can get involved in some injury (at work or out of work) and become a person with disability, which may last for a few weeks.

A few things that can benefit all, more so to people with disability, are to have ramps at places, a bar handle in the toilet, a staircase chair etc.

In India there are around 27 million people who have physical or mental disability making up for 2.2% of India's population. It is disheartening to see hardly any public place or an office friendly to their requirements.

A good employer should make reasonable adjustments and redesign the workplace to ensure workers with disability are able to move freely. Management should also ensure that person with disability doesn't face discrimination or barriers. A person with disability should be a part of every function or meeting like any other employee.

Ensuring good working conditions involves the following:

- Sharing good work practices with employees
    - How: Arrange a Townhall (meeting) and address the issue
    - Example: Taking frequent breaks while working
    - Benefits: Less fatigue and musculoskeletal problems at the end of the day
- Walkthrough rounds in the workplace
    - How: Senior managers form teams and walks through the workplace along with the team members

periodically to observe if work, workplace and working conditions are in accordance with good practices
  - Example: During a walkthrough in a workshop, it is observed that the place is stuffy and unkept
  - Benefits: Identify deficiencies and take remedial actions
- Training
  - How: Train employees in safe working
  - Example: Manual handling training for those whose job involves repeated lifting of heavy weights
  - Benefits: Employee doesn't get backache issues
- Investing in things that makes working efficient
  - How: By making the work (job) the equipment and the workplace fit the worker (ergonomics)
  - Example: Use of monitors, keyboard and mouse instead of working with laptops
  - Benefits: Less fatigue and musculoskeletal problems at the end of the day, both long term and short term
- Respecting each other
  - How: Be kind and polite in your conversations, especially arguments. Do not belittle or make fun of others, especially those who are sick due to a chronic disease or have disability
  - Example: Have out-of-work chats occasionally (about family, hobbies etc.)
  - Benefits: Develops trust and a great team
- Walk-the talk
  - How: Encourage respectful speak-up culture
  - Example: No victimization of those who speak up, respectfully
  - Benefits: Freedom to think, work, innovate etc.

Some basic ergonomics steps that can make all workers (including those with disability) and the work efficient:

- Encourage workers to take frequent breaks
  - A short break of even one minute can refresh you to continue your task efficiently
- Work in a neutral position
  - Keeping your arm close to the body is neutral position. Working in this position does not fatigue you as much as keeping your arm away from the body
- Keep regularly used materials within easy reach
  - It reduces fatigue as you are not overstretching to search frequently required materials
- Discourage use of excessive force
  - Using a trolley instead of shifting a heavy box manually reduces incidence of backache
- Work at a proper level
  - Not working at a proper level causes muscles to strain and cause early fatigue leading to performance issues and even accidents
- If job requires repetitive movements, take a break
  - Taking a break in jobs involving hammering, shifting packages or even working with computers breaks the monotony of the job as well as provides rest from repetitive tasks
- Work in adequately-spaced areas
  - Have enough elbow space and legroom to work with a clear view to prevent accidents
- Move often and stretch yourself
  - Sitting or standing for too long isn't good. If sitting for long, stand and move around and stretch. If standing for long, sit, relax and stretch.

- Minimize stressors at workplace
    - Heat, light, glare, noise, negativity (toxic culture) etc. are stressors which cause discomfort and distraction during work and additionally cause illnesses

As mentioned above, there are lot of areas where an Occupational Health (OH) physician can sensitize the management as some issues have potential to even cause mental health problems in vulnerable employees.

Disability can happen to anyone – a worker today can get involved in some injury (at work or out of work) and become a person with disability, which may last for a few weeks.

The OH physician should listen to employees who come for consultations and say that they have 'a feeling of being uncomfortable at workplace due to some people around' and proactively bring it to the attention of management. The HR (Human Resources) department should be involved after employee consent. Usually, the management will address such issues in appropriate forums.

Many offices have areas that are difficult to navigate even for people without disability. During walkthrough rounds these could be identified and improvements made to benefit all. During consultations with the OH physicians, employees may also talk about these difficult-to-navigate areas.

Although making the workplace safe to work so that no one develops any work-related illness or gets injured is a responsibility of all, employees should interact with OH physician, an Ergonomist as well as with Safety professionals to achieve this goal.

Work-Related (Occupational) Rheumatoid Arthritis

(published on 12th February, 2023 in www.occupationist.com)

A Swedish study suggests that workers exposed to airborne toxins may have an increased risk of developing rheumatoid arthritis (RA), an immune system disorder that causes swelling and pain in the joints.

The study found that among men, bricklayers, concrete workers, manual load handlers and electricians were at twice the risk or more to develop rheumatoid arthritis than if they would have been in certain other occupations. In women, nursing jobs had a 30% higher risk than other jobs.

Compared with men working desk jobs, electrical workers had twice the risk of rheumatoid arthritis and bricklayers and concrete workers had roughly triple the risk.

The lead author Anna Ilar of the Karolinska Institute in Sweden said, "Previous studies have indicated that occupations within the manufacturing sector are associated with an increased risk of rheumatoid arthritis."

Anna further emphasized, "The novelty of our findings is that we showed that occupations within this sector are related to an increased risk of rheumatoid arthritis even after controlling for lifestyle-related factors including smoking, alcohol use, education and obesity."

Smoking is a known risk factor for rheumatoid arthritis, but the findings of this study add to evidence suggesting that environmental factors could trigger the disease in some people engaged in jobs in such settings.

Earlier research suggested that lung changes caused by inhaled pollutants may trigger immune responses that lead to rheumatoid arthritis, particularly in individuals with a genetic predisposition for the disease.

For this study, researchers examined data on 3,522 people with rheumatoid arthritis and 5,580 similar individuals without the condition. Information was gathered on work history from questionnaires and results analyzed from blood samples looking for genetic factors that can contribute to the disorder.

Researchers compared the increased risk of rheumatoid arthritis in manufacturing occupations to the risk associated with professional, administrative and technical jobs that tend to involve deskwork rather than manual labor.

Compared with men working desk jobs, electrical workers had twice the risk of rheumatoid arthritis and bricklayers and concrete workers had roughly triple the risk.

The study didn't find an increased risk of rheumatoid arthritis for women working in the manufacturing sector, but this could be due to too few women in these jobs to properly analyze the impact of this work.

It's possible that inhaled toxins such as silica, asbestos, organic solvents and motor exhaust might have contributed to the development of rheumatoid arthritis, but the study didn't analyze which pollutants caused the condition.

One limitation of the study is that researchers assumed people in professional jobs in doing office work didn't have exposure to toxins that may increase the odds of rheumatoid arthritis. The study also wasn't a controlled experiment designed to prove whether or how certain occupations might cause rheumatoid arthritis.

Triggers to the immune system, both at home and workplace may increase the chance for an abnormal response by the immune system leading to any autoimmune disease, rheumatoid arthritis being one.

They also didn't directly examine the influence of manual labor on development of rheumatoid arthritis, said Kaleb Michaud, a researcher at the University of Nebraska Medical Center and co-director of the National Data Bank for Rheumatic Diseases.

Michaud, who wasn't involved in the study said, "There is some evidence that greater physical labor, which can cause more stress on the body physically and mentally, can lead to rheumatoid arthritis."

"Not getting enough sleep and continuous repetitive tasks can lead to added stress that can impact your immune system," Michaud added. "The more triggers to the immune system just increase the chances for an irregular response by it that may lead to an autoimmune disease like rheumatoid arthritis."

The study published in Arthritis Care and Research in 2017 alerts the Occupational Health (OH) physician to be vigilant to environmental factors as they could trigger a lot of health issues in the workers.

Rheumatoid arthritis (RA) is an autoimmune disease and autoimmune reactions may be provoked by harmful airborne exposures.

Despite the results presented in the study, the authors say there is still much to be done in order to understand the specifics of how certain work factors affect RA risk.

"It is important to point out that you will not necessarily develop rheumatoid arthritis just because you have had a certain occupation or have been exposed to potentially harmful exposures at work," said Ilar.

"But, airborne exposures may lead to a greater risk of rheumatoid arthritis," she added. "That is why it is important that findings on preventable risk factors are spread to employees, employers, and decision-makers in order to prevent disease by reducing or eliminating known risk factors."

The conclusion of the research so far is not to generate a fear among employees and employers as there is likelihood of many other factors that can cause or trigger development of rheumatoid arthritis but be mindful and reduce the known risk factors and find out unknown risk factors in order to prevent any chance of developing rheumatoid arthritis.

A program to identify and mitigate the threat to health by airborne particles should be established by the OH physician in both in offices and factories, especially as silica, asbestos, organic solvents and motor exhaust are known to negatively impact health. An Occupational Hygienist (Industrial Hygienist) can support such a program!

36

Work-life balance, politicians, and Occupational Health

(published on 31st January, 2023 in www.occupationist.com)

Jacinda Ardern, the 42-year-old Prime Minister (PM) of New Zealand, on 19th January 2023 announced her resignation citing that she no longer had 'enough in the tank' to continue leading her country. The resignation, she said, was not because the job was hard but because of time.

Whatever be the country's size, a Prime Minister's job has no working hours. And if the PM has no working hours, it applies for the core team of ministers too. It cascades down to the village level political head, the patwari or sarpanch (in India).

Experiencing burnout even in the job that you love is not uncommon.

Emergencies like terrorist activities, earthquakes, floods, riots etc. that threaten the nation often come unannounced and the politicians have to be ready for that, else their personal reputation is at stake.

Jacinda was New Zealand's PM for about 5 years. In some Asian countries and in Russia, it is not uncommon for politicians to complete decades in the highest office or in high offices and never feel strained about it. The job is harder if the population is larger and internal and external problems more complex, yet they enjoy it, don't appear ruffled and find time for it.

In India, the current PM Narendra Modi is known to work for at least 18 hours day after day. He supposedly takes no weekends and no vacations. He does no entertainment (including partying as it is called nowadays). Yet he seems to be enjoying the job and is the most respected leader in the world today.

Around 2000 AD, India had a PM, Atal Bihari Vajpayee, who would close shop at 6 pm and indulge in spending evening hours like a common man.

PM Modi works in the official aircraft as well. However, as early as in the 1960s it was not uncommon for the then Indian PM Late Lal Bahadur Shastri to be working in an aircraft.

No Indian PM has voluntarily left office or died due to work-life balance (WLB) issues. Three Indian PMs died in office, each one of them had a different reason of death but not WLB. In fact, in India very few politicians, big or small die in office or leave office due to WLB.

An important component of WLB is time. It is not only work, but the workplace and the working conditions that influence WLB. To name a few - happiness in what you are doing, freedom at work, flexi-hours, health and safety at workplace, monetary compensation etc. These days there is an earlier unheard component, namely, WFH (work from home) which also contributes to WLB.

The risks to work life balance should be managed well by all concerned, else the possibility of getting stressed due to the job one does will remain, eventually impacting health, quality of life, efficiency and productivity at work.

India has around 650,000 villages and each one has a political structure and support staff working in tough conditions, yet it is unheard about anyone resigning due to WLB issues.

Should the heads of State (the PMs, the Presidents etc.) entertain themselves to have work life balance?

Are politicians, especially the Indian politician different from the common man or do they enjoy their jobs better than the common man that WLB takes a backseat in the politicians or do they find time to de-stress.

Is WLB meant only for the common man or is it being fed into the minds of the common man by the preachers and media or is it that the common man doesn't enjoy the job? Or is WLB just a currently most talked about term.

In developing countries, especially, there is little control that the common man has on the contributory factors involved in WLB, like happiness in what you are doing, freedom to work, flexi-hours, working from home (WFH), monetary compensation etc. The risks to work life balance should be managed well, else the possibility of getting stressed due to the job one does will remain, eventually impacting health, quality of life, efficiency and productivity at work.

What does the resignation of Jacinda, the PM of New Zealand, mean to Indian politicians and the common man in India who are working in corporate offices and factories, both big and small, organized and unorganized?

For the common man, Jacinda's resignation signals that it is good to take proactive steps if you think you don't have the time to do the job, even if the job is hard and you are enjoying it. And to definitely take proactive steps if you are not enjoying the job. Taking proactive steps to your advantage is a stage just before burnout, and Jacinda didn't want to burnout. It was a personal decision and she wanted to spend time with her family. Her daughter was about to start school. It was more to do with 'quality of life' as she must have missed out on these things as a PM.

It is important for senior managers including C-suite executives to be aware of that if the job no more is enjoyable to themselves or if they sense it in their employees, proactive steps should be taken to avoid burnout. Proactive steps need not mean a resignation but practising time management and other stress management techniques. Experiencing burnout even in the job that you love is not uncommon.

This brings us to another question. Should the heads of State (the PMs, the Presidents etc.) entertain themselves to have WLB?

In August 2022, in a leaked video, Finland's PM Sanna Marin was seen singing and dancing with friends at a private party. Similar videos are seen in social media all over the world but the video leak of the 36-year old Sanna Marin triggered a debate in Finland if it was drugs being used in the party, if she was working or on vacation and was she sober enough to handle an emergency had one arose. People even asked if it was good for the PM to 'party'.

The Finnish PM Sanna Marin eventually took a drug test to end speculation about illegal drug abuse and said, "I hope that, in the year 2022, it's accepted that even decision-makers dance, sing and go to parties," Marin told reporters. "I didn't wish for any images to be spread, but it's up to the voters to decide what they think about it."

The author feels that it is a personal choice for the head of the state whether to 'party' or not.

The above examples point towards an understanding of mental health. An Indian politician is untouched by the pressure of work in a large country with complex issues. The PM of New Zealand proactively resigned citing lack of time. The PM of Finland was accused of partying and was seen as having fun, eventually stressing her; the very reason why she perhaps chose to party.

Could there be some advice to a head of the state from OH point of view? Very few Asian politician will ever reach out to any doctor for some advice on an issue like this because it exposes them as being weak which could mar their long-term prospects. However, if an OH physician is in the panel of doctors advising the head of the state, and one day he/she will be, the advice during conversations with the head of the state should be around taking time off in-between long meetings, sleeping in time, eating healthy, having short vacations, doing whatever it takes to de-stress oneself (including partying) etc.

The same advice is for the common man, with one difference – if you do not enjoy your job or the place of work, change. If the change of job requires upskilling, do it well in time. These are some of the proactive steps to manage stress, else it leads to burnout.

As mentioned earlier, it is good to take proactive steps if you think you don't have the time to do the job, or if the job is hard and even if you are enjoying it. And to definitely take proactive steps if you are not enjoying the job. Taking proactive steps to your advantage is a stage just before burnout.

Remember, experiencing burnout even in the job that you love is not uncommon.

www.ingramcontent.com/pod-product-compliance
Lightning Source LLC
LaVergne TN
LVHW041936070526
838199LV00051BA/2806